Jamaican born Patricia Cumper won a place on the Jamaica scholarship at Girton College, Cambridge. Patricia is also an award winning playwright, writing plays for the stage, including Royal Court theatre, BBC radio and television. One of her plays THE RAPIST has been published by Macmillan Caribbean Writers Series. Another play, THE KEY GUIDE was voted *Time Out*'s Critics choice.

ONE
ℬRIGHT
CHILD

A novel based on a true story by
PATRICIA CUMPER

BLACKAMBER BOOKS

ONE BRIGHT CHILD

Published by BlackAmber Books Limited
3 Queen Square, London WC1N 3AU
www.blackamber.com

First published by BlackAmber Books 1998

First reprint 1999

This revised edition 2004
Copyright © 1998 Patricia Cumper
Illustration © Peter Springer
All rights reserved

A CIP Catalogue record for this book is available in the British Library

ISBN: 1–901969–21–5

Typeset in 10/12 pt Plantin by
RefineCatch Limited, Bungay, Suffolk
Printed by WS Bookwell, Finland

$\mathscr{D}$EDICATION

In loving memory of my parents,
George Edward Cumper
(1923 – 1993)
and
Gloria Clare Cumper
(1922 – 1995)
and
to my son,
Andrew McKenzie,
for his patience and understanding.

ACKNOWLEDGEMENTS

Sincere thanks to Miss Enid Godwin, last headmistress of the Mary Datchelor School, and to the archivist at Girton College, Cambridge, for helping me understand the times and places in which the events of this book took place; to Reg Carpenter and Joyce Thomas for sharing their memories of their sister, Gloria; and to George and Gloria's many friends, particularly Leslie Rose and Antonia Shooter Rose for their support and kindness. Any mistakes are mine, and any liberties taken with the truth are my responsibility.

'We are part human, part stories.'

BEN OKRI
FROM *The Joys of Storytelling*, PHOENIX HOUSE

℘ROLOGUE

'IF A CERTAIN little girl is hiding up in this mango tree,' Father said between puffs on his pipe, 'she should think about comin' down now.' He stood at the foot of the largest tree in his garden.

A small rustling of the leaves over his head was his only reply. A hundred yards away, a tram rumbled past the house's imposing concrete gates, its lights winking through the rails of the iron fence which enclosed the smooth, rectangular lawn. Father drew on his pipe again, the heart of the bowl glowing in the moonlight. 'Your mother is not the mos' patient of women,' he added.

The tree frogs began peeping in the silence after his words. A smile stole over Father's face, making his teeth gleam in his dark face. He knocked the fire out of the bowl of his pipe against the tree trunk, placed his pipe carefully in the top pocket of his khaki shirt, then began to climb the mango tree.

Twenty feet up, he arrived at the fork in which his daughter was sitting. Small for her thirteen years, she sat dangling her legs over the branch, confident of her perch as a bird. Puffing a little, Father settled himself on a sturdy branch nearby.

'Those lights, Father – the ones by the harbour. You think that's our ship?' Gloria asked.

'Could be, child. Could be.'

Gloria sighed. 'Why do I have to go to school in England, Father?' she asked, the question forcing itself out of her. 'I didn't cheat in that exam. It wasn't my fault. I *didn't* cheat!'

1

'I know that, child.'

'Then why?'

'School in England is not punishment, child. Is a way of making a better life for you. If the teachers in Jamaica are too foolish to understand that you could know all the answers without cheating, then your mother and I decided to find you a school with less ignorant teachers.' Father spoke firmly, reassuringly, peering through the leaves to see the expression on his daughter's face as best he could. Her eyes, always expressive, were confused, frowning.

'But Mrs Shenton was English and she was the one that thought I cheated. Suppose all the teachers in England think—'

'You going to go to a good school, child. Your mother make sure of that. You just think of going to England as climbing a higher mango tree, mi love,' Father said. 'From there, you get to see half the world, not just Kingston Harbour.'

Gloria rewarded him with a small smile.

'Maybe I'll get to see the King. Or Mrs Simpson,' she said thoughtfully. Father smiled and nodded.

'Anyt'ing is possible,' he agreed.

In the house below, the front steps were bathed in light as the front door opened onto the generous verandah. The light slipped through the railing to pick out the red flowers in the hibiscus and monkey fiddle hedge that surrounded it. Mother, a slim, brown-skinned woman in her mid-forties, bustled onto the verandah, her friend and confidante, Mrs Marley, in tow. As Mrs Marley departed, retreating down the drive after a flurry of admonitions to take care, Mother turned to squint into the darkness of the garden.

'Don't try my patience tonight, young lady!' she said, her voice pitched at exactly the right volume to reach Gloria's ear. 'Or you and I will have serious words!'

Father chuckled.

'You go down first, Father,' Gloria pleaded. 'She won't quarrel so much if you go down first!'

'I wouldn't depend on *that*, mi love,' Father said, beginning the descent.

They stood side by side like naughty school children before Mother, eyes downcast. Gloria traced a circle in the cool dust with her big toe.

'And where are your shoes and stockings, Gloria?' Mother demanded.

Gloria looked desperately to Father, but he seemed deeply involved in repacking his pipe from a pouch he had fished out of his back pocket.

'I hate stockings,' she muttered as defiantly as she dared. 'They make me itch. And you can't climb a mango tree with shoes on.'

'Why must you behave like some chiggerfoot country girl?' Mother demanded. A small noise escaped Father's lips, but he fought valiantly to control it.

'And don't you dare even crack a smile, Will Carter. You will just encourage her.'

Glancing up with eyes full of laughter, he saw that Mother too was having difficulty maintaining her annoyance at her daughter. Fine looking woman, he thought to himself.

'I got her feet back on the ground, Mother. The rest is up to you,' he stated aloud. Striking a match on his boot, he lit his pipe and walked back to the house. Mother stood, arms akimbo, studying her daughter.

'Turning into a young lady and yet you see not one thing wrong with climbing up into a tree like any tomboy without the slightest concern that anybody who care to look could see your bloomers,' she said.

Gloria heard the softening of her voice and glanced up.

'I just wanted to take one last look at everything,' she said, then added mischievously, 'Besides, you and Mrs Marley were busy packing. You never even noticed I was gone.'

They began to walk back to the house.

'Removing all those books you put into our trunk, you mean,' Mother said.

'*David Copperfield*?' Gloria asked in growing panic. 'And *Pride and Prejudice*?'

Mother nodded.

'Even *Little Women*?'

Mother looked amused. 'You think you have one book that they don't have in England by the dozen?'

'I suppose so, but—'

'Does everything have to be a debate with you, child?' Mother asked in mock despair. She stopped, took Gloria's hand, made her look her in the eye. Gloria was startled. Her mother had never done this before.

'Listen to me, Gloria. An education is something nobody can ever take away from you. If you get an English education, not a soul would dare turn up their nose at you, question you in any way: the Governor himself will invite you to tea at Kings House.'

As quickly as it had come, the edge of anger disappeared from Mother's voice. 'Off to bed now. I want you looking fresh and pretty when we sail out of Kingston Harbour tomorrow morning.'

'Yes, Mother.'

As she went inside, Gloria ran her fingers along the wooden rail of the verandah, along the rough sand-dashed walls of the house, across the panes of frosted glass set in the door. She breathed deeply and thought she could smell the frangipani blooming at the bottom of the garden, and the last traces of the coconut oil that Cook had boiled over the wood fire in the outside kitchen that day. She pressed her bare feet into the smooth, red-stained wooden floors of the house as she made her way to her bedroom past the three sea trunks stacked in the passageway. Behind her, she heard the familiar routine of Mother locking the doors and turning out the lights before going to bed.

The window beside Gloria's bed shook gently as the midnight tram rumbled past the gate. She had often been to the docks with Father, sitting beside him in the Austin as he collected some friend or relative who had just arrived on the banana boat that docked at Victoria Pier. He would supervise the strapping of boxes and suitcases to the Austin's generous running boards. She would watch as the porters scurried to unload the trunks and crates, and the longshoremen swung crane-loads of goods onto the shore. She realized that this time it was her turn to go on board; she would be the one at the rail waving goodbye as the ship slid out into the harbour and around the Palisadoes sand spit. As she fell asleep, she wondered who would help Cook grate the dry coconuts to boil coconut oil, who would be small enough to slide into the fowl coop and bring out all the eggs without frightening the chickens the way she could. The tree frogs peeped relentlessly outside her window. Now and then the rough cry of a croaking lizard joined their chorus.

CHAPTER ONE

'I THOUGHT I would put the two of you in here, Mrs Carter. One of my nicest rooms.' Mrs Chagler grinned ingratiatingly, her broad pink face creased with the effort of maintaining a smile that never reached her eyes. 'I've aired it out special since I knew you were coming.' She smoothed her grey wool skirt with hands chapped with housework and ran a calculating, and rather watery blue eye over the sea trunks that two burly young men were carrying into the room.

Gloria looked around her, huddling deeper into the thick wool sweater, her only protection against the September chill. The room was large, with a great bay window filled with grimy sash-panes looking out onto the foggy street below. A creaky wooden floor was covered by a carpet that had seen better days. The wardrobe, desk and dressing table were massive and dark, devoid of the sheen of care. The bed was covered with a chenille spread more grey than white. Dust tickled Gloria's nose and she sneezed.

'You better wrap up warm – Gloria, is it? You don't want to be catching a cold this time of year, specially with a pea souper like today. It'll stay on your chest all winter. Happened to me last year. Dreadful.' Mrs Chagler looked to Mother for agreement, but found none, so dismissed the two lads who had taken to gawking at the two dark-skinned women with a bad-tempered wave of her hand.

'I don't have a cold,' Gloria said. 'It's the dust. Dust always makes me sneeze.'

Mrs Chagler's face tightened with annoyance. Mother tried to catch Gloria's eye.

'Dust? Nonsense! I cleaned this room myself,' Mrs Chagler replied, tart as vinegar.

'I'm sure this room will be quite fine, Mrs Chagler,' Mother said, soothingly.

'I'm going to have to charge you just a little bit more than I said in my letter, I'm afraid, seeing as how this room is bigger than the one I was going to put you in,' Mrs Chagler oozed, her smile as set as cold fat on mutton. 'As soon as I saw you arriving with those trunks, well, I realized I couldn't squeeze you in that old place, could I?'

'I thought you said you dusted it before we got here, not after you saw how big our trunks were,' Gloria challenged.

'I dust *all* my rooms – all the time!' Mrs Chagler snapped, then remembered to smile. 'Smart as a whip, this little one, Mrs Carter. Nothing gets past her.'

Mother looked reprovingly at Gloria.

'She just wants to charge us more money,' Gloria replied, unabashed.

'Gloria!' The girl knew that warning note in her mother's voice so retired to examine the furniture and peer out the window. 'We have two more trunks to come, Mrs Chagler. Would you have them brought up for me when they arrive?'

'Of course, Mrs Carter.'

Then, instead of leaving as Mother expected, Mrs Chagler held out her hand.

'I hate to worry you, but the men are expecting a little gratuity for their trouble, those sea trunks ain't exactly as light as a feather. It's better if I pay, them being somewhat unscrupulous and wanting to take advantage of you ... colonials,' she apologized.

Mother opened her purse and began to extract some coins.

'It happened once before,' the woman went on, 'but I don't

let my boarders be taken advantage of any more, I can tell you. Most people won't do it, of course,' she said, watching the coins drop into her palm, 'but I've taken in visitors like yourself for the last ten years, Mrs Carter, and never had a complaint.'

With the expertise of long practice, she knotted the coins in her handkerchief and thrust it up her sleeve, then made for the door.

'So, welcome to London and Mrs Chagler's Boarding House for Ladies. I hope you'll be very happy here!'

As the door closed behind their landlady, Mother went to sit on the bed, an expression of determined cheerfulness on her face.

'Well, here we are, Gloria – in London. Now, isn't this nice?' she said, then sneezed loudly as a cloud of dust rose off the chenille bedspread to tickle her nose.

'Please stop fidgeting with that uniform, Gloria. You look fine!'

Exasperated, Mother removed Gloria's gloved hand from the collar she had been tugging at ever since getting dressed that morning. She pulled her daughter's navy coat into place so it lay smoothly on her shoulders, and tweaked one of the corkscrew curls she had coaxed into being with a hot comb, back into place. She straightened the blue serge hat on her daughter's head, then sat back in the taxi and looked out at the trees shedding their russet leaves on the misty streets.

'You remember what I told you? You say "Yes . . ."?'

'Yes, please,' Gloria intoned.

'And "No . . ."?'

'No, thank you.'

'That's how educated people talk, so don't forget – you hear me?'

'Yes, Mother. But why do I have to—?'

The taxi driver slid the panel back, as the taxi began to pull into the kerb.

'Here we are, love. The Mary Datchelor.'

'Pull over by the main gates, please,' Mother said, opening her purse.

Gloria's finger returned to tugging at her collar. A stream of girls, all dressed in the same dark coat, gloves and hat as herself, were making their way towards the school gates. Many pairs of curious eyes turned towards the girl getting out of the taxi, her skin shone so darkly against the scrap of white blouse which showed at the neck of her coat.

'Don't believe in educating girls m'self,' the cabdriver remarked as he took payment. 'That Mrs Simpson is supposed to be an educated woman and look at the trouble she's causing. Abdication? For a woman? Rubbish!'

As the taxi spluttered off into the mist, Mother turned to face the main gate, shoulders back and chin up. Taking Gloria's hand, she headed for the imposing front door with determined steps, as if she hadn't noticed the sudden silence their presence caused as they entered the Mary Datchelor School for Girls.

'You just remember to look them right in the eye, Gloria,' she muttered. '*Right in the eye!*'

Where Gloria was small and dark, Elizabeth Warren was the complete opposite. Gangling and awkward, her blonde hair hung in a thick, uneven plait behind her, scraped back off a plain face. She smiled and her whole face lit up as she burst through the door of the headmistress's office.

'You wanted to see me, Miss Brock?' she asked, looking in open curiosity at Gloria and her mother.

'Yes, I did, dear. Elizabeth, this is Gloria. She will be joining your class. Would you be kind enough to show her around the school for me?'

'Yes, Miss Brock. Come on, Gloria. We'll start with the library. And then we can go to the music room. I'm not terribly musical, but Miss Donnington lets me help organize the sheet-music for the school orchestra – and oh, we can take a look at where they're going to build the swimming pool, if you like . . .'

Gloria followed this benevolent whirlwind into the corridors of the school. As the door closed behind them, Mother nodded with satisfaction.

'I thought perhaps we could have a little chat, Mrs Carter. While Elizabeth shows Gloria around,' Miss Brock ventured.

'You have a very nice school here, Miss Brock. Very English,' Mother said.

'Thank you. We take a certain pride in it,' the headmistress replied. 'Do you think Gloria will find it easy to adjust?'

'She has no choice in the matter, Miss Brock.'

'We have girls who come to us here from all over the country, all over the world. Homesickness can sometimes be—'

'I will be staying in England to see that she gets a good start, Miss Brock,' Mother said firmly. Seeing that the other woman was still not satisfied, she added, 'If it is a matter of money . . .?'

'No, no, don't get me wrong, I beg you. We are delighted to have Gloria here.' Mother permitted herself a small, relieved smile. 'My brother worked for a while in Jamaica and he said that the schools there maintain more than acceptable standards, so I was somewhat curious as to why . . .?'

'May I speak my mind, Miss Brock?' Mother opened her handbag and extracted a framed photograph. She passed it to the headmistress.

'Of course, Mrs Carter.'

'My father was Scottish, Miss Brock. All my life my mother told me to say I was white. She was a mulatto and she would

stay home so that people wouldn't see how dark she was –
so I could pass for white, you see. And I did, Miss Brock. For
a while. Until I met my husband. That is a picture of my
husband, Miss Brock. Of Will Carter. He is a coloured man
and Gloria took his colouring, not mine.

'My Will is a chartered surveyor, Miss Brock, a decent,
hard-working man, but he never had money to spend until he
took himself a white partner in his business. It was my Will
that tramped the countryside surveying until his boots rubbed
his feet raw. His partner went to tea at Kings House and horse
races at Knutsford Park, but it was Will who made the money.
I say that to say this: if Gloria stayed in Jamaica, the best
schools couldn't change her colour. All her father's money
won't change the way people look at her. When she gets
full marks they will say it is because she cheated, because no
coloured child is supposed to be that bright. If she comes here
to this school, gets an English education, then people will have
to respect her, Miss Brock. And that is what she is here to get.'

Miss Brock returned the photograph and sat looking
thoughtful.

'If you don't want Gloria here, you are please to say so,'
Mother said firmly.

'Of course she must stay with us,' Miss Brock said, meeting
Mother's determined eyes with equal certainty. Mother gave
herself a silent prayer of thanks.

'Good,' she said. 'Now, would you be so kind as to tell me
where I can get a viola for Gloria? Her old one warped in the
sea air on the boat coming over and I am not going to let all
those years of private lessons go to waste!'

'Any chance of a cup of tea, Mrs Chagler?' Mother asked,
poking her head around the kitchen door. She had decided to
stop by the kitchen after picking up Gloria from school, drawn
not so much by the idea of tea but by the knowledge that it

was the only truly warm room in the house, and the days were growing steadily colder and colder, the darkness drawing down earlier and earlier.

Mrs Chagler wiped her hands on her ample cotton apron and hastily stubbed out the cigarette she had had hanging from her bottom lip as she prepared the dinner.

'Come in, come in, Mrs Carter. There's a pot of tea on the stove.'

Mother entered, removing the small cloche hat she had anchored to her head with a long hatpin. A reluctant Gloria came in behind her, her school coat buttoned firmly up to her chin, and sat in the nearest chair she could find to the oven. She stretched her hands towards its warmth.

'So how do you find your new school, Gloria?' Mrs Chagler asked, pouring three cups of strong, dark tea.

'Everybody knows everybody else and I don't know anybody, and they all stop and stare at me every time I walk past. They keep the windows open in the classrooms and I was so cold today I couldn't feel my pencil in my hand.' The words tumbled out despite her mother's quelling look.

'It's just her first week, Mrs Chagler. I'm sure she will learn to be happy there eventually. It's a very good school. Very advanced.'

'Must be costing you a pretty penny,' Mrs Chagler suggested, sitting to drink her tea at the sturdy wooden table that occupied the middle of the kitchen. Mother sipped her tea and hoped her face didn't show how bitter it tasted to her.

'You can't put a price on education,' she said.

'No, no, of course not, but if you had to . . .' Mrs Chagler left the question hanging in the air. Gloria watched with curiosity the way she always stuck her little finger into the air when she raised the tea cup to her lips.

'Do you always cook our dinner yourself?' Gloria asked.

'Most evenings. Yes, I do.'

'England is a very peculiar place,' she said.

'Gloria!' Mother said warningly.

'Well, it is, Mother. Because you would never sit in the kitchen with Cook in Jamaica. You used to get upset if I even grated coconut with Cook, and I only used to do that because her eyes were getting dark and—'

'*Gloria!*'

Mrs Chagler struggled to smile. 'It's all right, Mrs Carter. She doesn't understand how these things are yet. But don't you worry,' she said, getting up to check one of the saucepans on the stove, 'she will. She soon will.'

Gloria looked across at her mother, a little crestfallen.

'Do I have to go back to school tomorrow?' she asked.

'Was anybody rude to you?' Mother asked.

'No, but . . .'

'Did you understand what the teacher was saying?'

'Yes, but . . .'

'Then count yourself lucky, young miss.' Mother rose, gathering up her hat and handbag. 'Dinner is at seven as usual, Mrs Chagler?' she asked, and when their landlady nodded, unable to speak because she was trying to light another cigarette off the stove, she took her daughter's hand and marched out of the kitchen whose warm air was layered with a week of cooking smells, into the cold and musty hallway which led to the stairs and to their chilly, uninviting room.

CHAPTER TWO

'ELIZABETH! GLORIA! OVER here!' Ruth Green's voice rang out over the hubbub of the school dining hall. She sat at the head of one of the long tables, smiling broadly if not pleasantly at Elizabeth and Gloria as they entered; ranged on either side of her were half a dozen smirking girls.

'Ignore her,' Elizabeth hissed in Gloria's ear. 'There are two seats at that other table over there.'

'I saved these seats 'specially for you,' Ruth called. Her cohorts tittered.

'I don't mind sitting with Ruth,' Gloria said.

'She's had it in for you ever since you came here,' Elizabeth muttered as they made their way to Ruth's table. 'I wish I was a boy. I'd punch her in the nose!'

'You sit beside me, Gloria,' Ruth said, as Elizabeth tried to sit down. 'I said I want Gloria to sit beside me, Elizabeth. Don't you have a science class to go to, or something?' Small-boned and slim, with dark hair that fell into gleaming waves, Ruth had the effect of unnerving Elizabeth, who at fourteen had not yet masterd the art of dressing her thick hair into any style that lasted more than fifteen minutes. Just to stand beside Ruth was to remind Elizabeth of all her shortcomings.

'Just because you play in the orchestra, you think you belong on Mount Olympus, looking down on the rest of us . . .' Elizabeth began, heatedly.

'Miss Brock would be so pleased, Elizabeth!' Ruth cut her off. 'A Greek reference – very impressive.' She turned to

Gloria, shutting Elizabeth out. 'I need you to settle a dispute for me, Gloria. You see – we don't know what to call you.' A conspiratorial smirk slid round Ruth's companions. 'Jane says you are coloured, but Sandy says you should say Negro and Jilly has an uncle in Australia and she says they say blackfellow there.'

Gloria frowned thoughtfully as the girls waited expectantly.

'Call me Gloria,' she said at last.

'I didn't mean your name,' Ruth snapped. 'I meant how do we say what you are?'

'I told you,' Gloria said. 'I am Gloria. If you want to describe me to someone, *you* find the word.'

'Bravo!' chortled Elizabeth. The other girls looked to Ruth for guidance. Her forehead was wrinkled with a petulant frown.

'Oh, shut up, Elizabeth!' was all she could come up with. Elizabeth grinned as she began to dig into the creamed chicken and boiled potatoes that were growing cold on her plate. Ruth rose, tossing her fork onto her half-eaten lunch. The other girls kept their eyes on their food.

'The two of you belong together, you really do!' She flicked Elizabeth's blonde hair contemptuously. 'Silly haystack!' she said as her Parthian shot.

Gloria sat, knees tucked under her chin, in the middle of her bed at Mrs Chagler's Boarding House for Ladies. Two large sea trunks were open on the floor and Mother bustled about folding, wrapping, sorting the clothes and shoes she was packing into them.

'You knew I couldn't stay with you for ever, child,' she said firmly, wrapping a delicate silk blouse in layers of tissue paper before stowing it in one of the trunk's drawers. 'Father needs me home now. He's going to find himself a new wife if I don't get home soon. Six months is a long time to be away. That's the longest your father and I have ever been parted.' She picked up a pair of sturdy boots, and stood stroking them absentmindedly.

'Let me come home with you then. Please, Mother.' Bright tears stood in Gloria's eyes. Mother glanced at her, then began packing decisively again.

'Don't talk foolishness, child. You just pass me those blouses, please.'

Gloria climbed reluctantly off the bed. Made in fine cotton lawn and decorated with drawn threadwork and slip-stitched embroidery, the blouses were piled on the seat of an ancient armchair from which two or three tufts of horsehair protruded at the well-worn edges. Even after they had been laundered, the blouses still smelt faintly of the lavender eau de cologne Mother wore.

'I hate this place. I hate school,' Gloria said, delivering the blouses.

'My shoes now please, one pair at a time,' Mother ordered.

'And people look at me strangely everywhere I go,' Gloria continued, gathering an armful of shoes.

'One pair at a time, Gloria! I don't want everything falling about during the voyage.'

'They think I am stupid at school,' Gloria began, delivering a pair of brown kid shoes with instep straps caught with tortoiseshell buttons.

'Don't talk foolishness. Miss Brock says you are doing very well.' The brown shoes disappeared into one of the many drawers into which the interior of the trunk was divided.

'– For a coloured girl. They treat me like it is some sort of miracle I can keep up with the class, and then when I do something right, they praise me so much, the other girls don't like it. I hate it there.'

Mother closed the trunk drawer with a snap and turned to

face her daughter. She looked at her with narrowed eyes for a moment or two.

'Is that how you pay Father and I back for all our trouble?' she asked.

Gloria looked down at her toes, unable to meet her mother's steady gaze.

'It's not just school – it's everything. The cold and the way everything looks so dead in winter . . .'

'We saw those crocuses this morning – spring will soon be here.'

'. . . And the fog and how even when the sun shines it's always cold and everything looks grey and dirty. It's not the way I imagined! It's not England like the one I read about in all my books – except maybe *Oliver Twist*. You have to wear so many clothes all the time, I feel like an elephant, they are so heavy and—' Gloria drew breath and looked up at her mother. 'I miss Father. And Cook. And my mango tree.'

'If you want good, you' belly haffi run now and then, child. That's what your grandmother always used to say to me,' Mother replied quellingly.

'She didn't leave you in some horrible old school!' Gloria cried.

'I wish she had,' Mother rejoined with asperity. 'I wish she had, instead of letting me run wild in the country!'

'I hate Mrs Chagler! She smells and she keeps asking me how come my collars are so clean, as if she thinks my colour is going to rub off. And she pinches me when you are not looking!'

'Don't exaggerate, Gloria!' For the first time there was a note of real annoyance in Mother's voice. 'Now you just listen to me. You are going to go and spend your holidays with my friend Mrs Thompson in Southampton.'

'With who?' Gloria looked puzzled.

'Of course you remember Mrs Thompson. We went to tea with her at the Russian Tea Room, remember? She married that nice Englishman who used to be rector at St Andrew's Parish Church.'

'The one in Jamaica?'

'You know any other St Andrew's Parish Church?'

'You mean the lady with all the feathers on her hat?'

'That's the one.' Gloria looked gloomy at the realization. 'She was just like you,' Mother coaxed. 'She came here to live with Reverend Thompson and she found it very strange at first. But she settled in. I'm sure she'll be happy to tell you about it.' Mother resumed packing her trunks, rolling pairs of cotton stockings into neat, stowable bundles.

'But I don't want to settle in. I want to go home with you,' Gloria muttered, disheartened.

'I've written her address down on a piece of paper and put it in the front of your Bible, but if you lose it, Mrs Chagler has it too. Make sure you write Mrs Thompson and tell her when term is over so she can send you your ticket.' Gloria nodded glumly. 'Write home every week. Rain or shine.' Another small nod, then the sound of a stifled sob.

'I'll change. Please, I won't climb the mango tree and I won't read so much and I don't care if the teachers think I am cheating and I will keep my frocks clean and wear shoes all the time. *Please*. And I won't argue any more.'

Mother produced a linen handkerchief from her cuff in the twinkling of an eye and wiped away the two renegade tears that slid down her daughter's face.

'Go and call Mrs Chagler. I need to talk to her for a few minutes,' she said briskly.

'Mother, please.' Gloria's voice was a whisper.

'Hurry up, child. I don't have all afternoon!'

As the door closed behind her daughter, Mother used the same square of white linen to wipe away the tear that ran down her own cheek. She noticed, as she tucked the hand-kerchief away, that her hands were shaking ever so slightly.

'It's for the best and don't ever forget that, Albertha Carter,' she muttered to herself. She sat on the bed, staring past her trunks out of the grimy window to the grey sky beyond. 'All for the best.'

'Time to wake up, Gloria. I'm terribly sorry, but you're going to have to move to another room.' Mrs Chagler stood, arms folded across her ample chest, smiling as the girl huddled beneath her bedcovers, blinking sleepily in the dim dawn light.

'What? What other room? What time is it?'

'Past seven. Time for lazy young girls to be out of bed anyway. You'll be late for school.'

Mrs Chagler set about gathering Gloria's clothes and books into a large pile.

'Got a very important young lady coming in today, paying me good money for my best room,' she said, bustling about. Gloria climbed out of bed and stood shivering in her flannel nightdress, watching her.

'You can't move me out of this room. My mother paid for me to have it!' She grabbed the dresses Mrs Chagler was pulling from the wardrobe and began to hang them back up again.

'Oh, she paid for your board and lodging all right, but I can't remember ever saying that you would always be in this exact room,' Mrs Chagler said, snatching the dresses back again.

'I am not leaving this room!' Gloria declared, then sat determinedly in the middle of the floor, pulling in whatever of her possessions were nearest to her, then hugging them to her chest.

'Oh yes, you are, my girl!' Mrs Chagler huffed. 'I asked you politely.'

'This is my room!'

Mrs Chagler leant down and grabbed a handful of the pinafore Gloria was clutching and began dragging it away from her. Gloria clung to it like a drowning sailor to a barrel.

'Not ... any ... more ... it ... ain't!' The landlady emphasized her words with vigorous tugs on the pinafore. Gloria pulled back as hard as she could. Taken by surprise, Mrs Chagler slipped and landed with a bump on her ample backside. Her face flushed absolutely purple.

'Why, you little heathen!' she shouted. 'You did that on purpose, you did.' Any attempt at gentility had completely disappeared from her speech and posture.

'Serves you right!'

'What did you say?'

Rising with difficulty from the floor, she grabbed Gloria by the neck of her nightdress, hauling her to her feet and eventually onto her toes. She thrust her face into Gloria's and the girl fought not to recoil from the odour of stale cigarettes and cheap perfume.

'You did that deliberately, you did. Now pick up your things. I said *pick them up!*' Cowed by the hate in her voice, Gloria did as she was told. 'I do you people a favour letting you stay here when others wouldn't, and this is how you repay me,' she growled. 'Well, guess who is going to have to do all their own laundry from now on!'

Loading her arms with the clothes that Gloria could not carry, she shoved the shivering girl in front of her towards the door.

'I'll teach you to have some respect for your elders and betters!' she muttered. 'Too bloody smart for your own good!'

★ ★ ★ ★ ★

Gloria found the echoing silence of the school library comforting. Spring sunshine sent splashes of colour dancing across the books and tables from the tall stained-glass windows which ran along the length of the room.

'Miss Brock wants you in her office, Gloria,' Ruth hissed suddenly beside Gloria's ear. 'Writing home again?' she asked before Gloria could hide the letter under her textbook. 'Let me see that!'

The librarian looked up disapprovingly from her desk at the other end of the room. Ruth snatched the envelope and began to read the address.

'Give that back to me, Ruth!' Gloria whispered.

'Mrs A.T. Carter, HalfWay Tree Post Office . . .' Ruth snorted with laughter, prompting another sharp look from the librarian. 'Is that where your mum lives? In a tree?'

Gloria snatched at the letter but Ruth danced back, pulling it out of her reach. 'Are all the post offices in Jamaica in trees?'

'Would you two girls please be quiet!' the librarian said, her voice ringing in the large room. 'I'm surprised at you, Gloria Carter. This is most out of character.'

'I said give it back,' Gloria said, loudly and clearly. The librarian frowned at Ruth, watching both girls. Ruth threw the letter back onto the library table.

'Why on earth would I want to keep your stupid letter? Take it,' she said. 'After all, I am not the one keeping Miss Brock waiting,' she threw over her shoulder as she flounced out.

'Close the door behind you, Gloria. We need to have a little talk.'

Miss Brock was standing at the window of her office, looking out over the school gardens. Instead of resuming her accustomed seat behind her large mahogany desk, she went to sit in one of the armchairs beside a small fireplace. She indicated that Gloria should sit opposite. As upright as her mother had always instructed her to be, Gloria perched at the edge of the seat.

She's grown since she's been here, Miss Brock thought, looking at her. Not just taller, but as a person. Such direct eyes she has, she mused, and so wary for one so young.

'Some of your teachers are concerned about you, my dear. They seem to think you are a little . . .' Miss Brock hesitated and chose her word carefully. '. . . unkempt.' There was a short silence.

'I try to press these stupid uniforms, but I can't seem to get it right,' Gloria said. She gave Miss Brock a small ironic smile. 'I never had to do it at home, you see. Zilla did all our ironing for us. Mother used to say you could cut your finger on the creases in Father's trousers.' Her hands stroked the navy blue skirt, as if she hoped she could make good some of her mistakes. Miss Brock noticed for the first time small bags under Gloria's eyes, a tiny tremor in her hands.

'Do you know, there is another student who wants to come to Mary Datchelor and is looking for a place to lodge as her family live in Yorkshire. Would you mind if I came back to Mrs Chagler's with you, Gloria? It would be an ideal place for her to stay.'

Alarm chased surprise across Gloria's face.

'I was going to study in the library this afternoon, Miss Brock.'

'You know, the more I think about it, the more I like the idea of taking a good look at Mrs Chagler's Boarding House for Ladies.' The headmistress rose to her feet and smiled reassuringly at the girl looking uncertainly at her from the large armchair. 'Fetch your satchel and coat, Gloria. I shall be in the hall.'

Gloria felt as if she were seeing the hallway of Mrs Chagler's boarding house through Miss Brock's eyes as they entered, as if she were seeing it for the first time: the dust on the banister, the faded carpet on the uneven wooden floorboards, even the daffodils in the glass vase on the hall table which drooped as if tired of trying to suck up the chalky water whose residue dulled the inside of the vase.

'Is that you, Gloria?' Mrs Chagler called from the kitchen as the heavy front door closed behind Gloria and Miss Brock. 'You're home early. Don't expect your tea any time soon, my girl. I've been busy this afternoon and I haven't got around to it yet.'

Shepherding Gloria ahead of her, Miss Brock made her way towards the kitchen.

'Is that the way you speak to all the girls who are in your care, Mrs Chagler?' Miss Brock asked as she entered, her accent, Gloria noticed, even more precise than when she read out the morning lesson at school assembly. Mrs Chagler, sitting at the kitchen table, did not look up from the magazine in which she was engrossed.

'And who is asking?' she said, a half-smoked cigarette dancing as it remained firmly stuck to her bottom lip.

'This is Miss Brock, Mrs Chagler. My headmistress,' Gloria said. The cigarette disappeared under the table and the magazine was lowered immediately. Mrs Chagler then got to her feet, a deferential smile clambering up her features.

'Yes, yes, of course. Miss Brock. Mrs Carter told me all about you. Lovely school you have. All those girls learning. Lovely.'

'We take a great interest in the welfare of our pupils.' Miss Brock removed her kid gloves and looked around the kitchen, her face impassive, her eyes taking in every detail.

'A young girl like Gloria needs a firm hand, that's what her mother said to me when she left and I've been like a mother to her ever since Mrs Carter left and she's lying if she says any different!' Mrs Chagler gabbled.

Miss Brock turned that observant gaze on Mrs Chagler herself. 'Gloria has not said a word about you, Mrs Chagler. It was Mrs Carter who wrote and said she was concerned about her daughter.'

'Trying to get me in trouble, are you, writing spiteful little letters?' Mrs Chagler demanded of Gloria, her face flushing redder and redder by the second.

'I never said anything. Honest!' Gloria protested.

'I am very curious to know why Gloria is ironing her own school uniform,' Miss Brock said.

'She knows why! The little beast pulled me down, didn't she – hurt my back. Wouldn't do as she was told. I couldn't let her get away with that, now could I? It was just to teach her a lesson, that's all!' Mrs Chagler continued to glare at the girl.

'Gloria?' Miss Brock enquired.

'I'd do it again,' she muttered, glancing defiantly at Mrs Chagler.

'You see what I have to put up with, Miss Brock?'

'I liked that room. I wanted to stay in that room,' Gloria blurted out. There was a moment's silence as Miss Brock looked from the red-faced woman to the angry girl.

'You mean you've been moved out of the room in which you were staying? Would you care to explain why, Mrs Chagler? I presume this is the same room for which Mrs Carter is paying?'

'I needed it for a special visitor,' the woman said sulkily. 'It's too big for one little girl, Miss Brock. And some of the other lodgers don't take it too kindly when the likes of her takes up the best room in the house.' Even Mrs Chagler couldn't fail to notice Miss Brock's face contract with anger.

24

'Besides, I thought she would like it somewhere cosier,' she said, trying to mollify the headmistress.

'Do you mind if I take a look at this *cosy* room of yours, Gloria? I'm sure your mother would be interested to know what it looks like.'

Mrs Chagler's defiance deflated to apology.

'Of course I intended to put her back in the big room as soon as I could,' she began. Gloria's eyebrows shot up in surprise at this.

'Would this evening be too soon?' Miss Brock asked, her voice dangerously calm.

'This evening? But ...!' Mrs Chagler's protests died as Miss Brock cocked her head questioningly at her.

'Then you see, I could write to Mrs Carter and tell her that there was no longer any reason for her to worry and that Gloria was well looked after.'

Defeated, Mrs Chagler headed for the door. As she retreated down the hall and up the stairs, she could be heard muttering to herself: '... lucky to be staying in a boarding house as nice as this ... stirring up trouble for decent hard-working people ...'

As Miss Brock began putting on her gloves. Gloria tried hard to contain the huge smile that threatened to break out across her face.

'Why didn't you say something before, Gloria?'

'I was ashamed, I suppose. I really did pull her down. I thought I would get into trouble.'

'I think you will find that there are other ways of standing up for yourself, of fighting for what you want, my dear.' She smiled at the girl who stood in front of her, so straight, so upright, with that plain face and eyes that missed nothing.

'Thank you, Miss Brock,' Gloria said.

'Not at all, Gloria. I rather enjoyed it, I must confess. My father always said to me that if I'd been born a boy, I'd have made a first-class barrister, you know.' She smiled. 'It wasn't possible when I was a girl, of course – not like nowadays. Nowadays, Gloria, all sorts of things are possible.'

CHAPTER THREE

THE GREAT WINDOWS of the school dining hall were cocked open, allowing a cool summer breeze to blow through the room. Red-faced from a vigorous physical education lesson, Elizabeth was tucking happily into a bowl of stewed rhubarb generously laced with custard. Gloria watched her single minded efforts with amusement while Ruth, as immaculately groomed as ever in the pale blue summer dress and buff-coloured cotton lisle stockings that were the school's summer uniform, looked on in horror. Elizabeth mumbled something inaudible.

'Didn't anyone ever teach you not to talk with your mouth full, Elizabeth?' Ruth asked.

'Ignore her, Elizabeth,' Gloria retorted. 'What did you say?'

Elizabeth swallowed mightily. 'I said that my uncle is a barrister and he goes to the Old Bailey and Chambers and has lots of cases. Why are you asking about barristers all of a sudden?'

Before Gloria could reply, Ruth leapt in. 'That's not what barristers do, silly. Barristers defend people when they go to court – like murderers and robbers and such!'

Elizabeth scraped the last of the custard out of the bottom of her bowl. 'I was going to say that as well, if you'd given me a chance!'

'Why do you want to know anyway, Gloria?' Ruth asked, pointedly ignoring Elizabeth.

'I find it interesting, that's all,' Gloria said, getting up from the table. 'I think I'll go and look it up in the library after school.'

'Why on earth would she want to do that?' Ruth demanded of Elizabeth. 'We have exams in two weeks and rehearsals for the school orchestra every night – isn't that enough?' Elizabeth shrugged.

As she walked from the hall Gloria noticed not for the first time how odd the buff-coloured stockings made her legs look; she thought how wonderful it would feel to have real sunshine, not this weak imitation, but *real* sunshine on her own dark skin again.

Gloria became of aware of Mrs Chagler's presence in her room when the door banged against the wall. The landlady stood framed in the doorway, arms akimbo, glaring at the girl who sat by the window trying to catch the last of the summer light on the book she was reading.

'You've missed your supper again, and if you think I'm bringing it up here to you on a tray, you can perish that thought,' she stated belligerently. Gloria looked up reluctantly, marking her place in her text with her finger.

'I'm not hungry, Mrs Chagler. I ate a big lunch at school,' she said very calmly. She looked back down to the page, but Mrs Chagler had stepped into the room and was looking around her with curiosity.

'What do you find to read in those books that's so very interesting anyway, locked away up here all the time?' she said, trying to start up a conversation. She was staring in fascination at three shopping bags and a white cotton summer dress that lay across Gloria's bed. 'New dress, is it? And from Harrods, no less. It's all right for some of us with money to burn. Some of us have to work for our living.' As she reached for the dress, Gloria snatched it away, taking it to the wardrobe.

'If you don't mind?' she said. 'I needed a dress for the school recital.'

She hung the dress carefully on a heavy wooden hanger, shaking it gently so that the lace collar and trim fell into place.

'If you don't ma-ind . . .' mocked Mrs Chagler. 'Ain't we coming over all posh. You mark my words, Gloria Carter, this world is a hard place and there's no room in it for darkies with too much ambition.'

Gloria felt a knot of anger gather in her shoulders but she forced herself to hang up the dress and turn to face Mrs Chagler with the appearance of calm.

'Like Jesse Owens, you mean?'

'Anybody can run. Running is just running, isn't it? Don't see what Herr Hitler got so upset about, myself,' Mrs Chagler retorted.

'Or Learie Constantine?'

'Who do you think taught him everything he knows about cricket?' Mrs Chagler was beginning to enjoy herself.

'Or Billie Holiday?'

'Drinks like a fish. I can hear it clear through the wireless!'

Gloria paused, thoughtful. Then: 'So what about Mary Mcleod Bethune?'

Mrs Chagler's mouth shut with a snap. 'Never heard of her,' she said after a pause.

'She's only a coloured woman who advises President Roosevelt in America,' Gloria said, with a small triumphant smile.

'You made that up!' Mrs Chagler charged. 'You couldn't think of anything so you made that up!'

Gloria went back to her seat and took up her textbook again.

'Look it up if you don't believe me,' she suggested, her eyes already on the page.

'I will.'

'I need to do my homework, Mrs Chagler.'

The landlady's chapped cheeks flushed red at the polite but dismissive note in the young woman's voice.

'I tell you what, Gloria. When you go back to Jamaica, you can leave those dresses here for some *decent* people to wear!' She threw the words over her ample shoulder as she marched from the room, slamming the door behind her.

The light had become too dim for Gloria to read easily so she tucked her feet up under her on the window seat and watched the people on the street below going about their evening business: a young couple walking together, her hand tucked behind his elbow; a middle-aged man with a handle-bar moustache striding briskly along; a couple of small boys in breeches and short jackets, tumbling energetically down the street after a red, India-rubber ball.

'Move out of the doorway, Elizabeth. You take up twice as much room as everybody else as it is!' Ruth Green sneered as she slipped past Elizabeth back to her seat. Miss Brock was late for class and Ruth had taken the opportunity to go to the cloakroom and touch up her already immaculate hair.

'No, she doesn't, Ruth,' Gloria spoke up.

'And how would *you* know, Gloria? You come from Half-Way Tree.'

'Leave her alone, Ruth!' This time it was Elizabeth's turn to spring to Gloria's defence. The two had become firm friends in the two years that Gloria had been at Mary Datchelor, a friendship that Ruth viewed with both scorn and envy and which she tried at intervals to sabotage, so far with little success.

'What I want to know is how someone who lived in a tree speaks English so well. She's so very clever that she can even play the viola. Miss Brock thinks she plays ever so well.' Ruth's voice was pitched just loud enough that the rest of the class could hear. Her remarks were rewarded with a few titters.

'Ever so well,' she continued, 'for someone who *lives in a tree.*'

Ruth looked at Gloria triumphantly and was pleased but not a little surprised to see that the other girl was hanging her head in shame. Gloria gave a little sigh.

'I suppose you would have found out the truth anyway,' she said, 'so I might as well tell you.'

Ruth crowed with triumph. 'See? See? I told you something wasn't right!' She turned to face Gloria, her face alight with curiosity. Several other of the girls came and stood around too.

'It was . . . missionaries. I can't fool you any more. I lived in a tree – my whole family lived in a mango tree. The missionaries taught us to speak English, made us read the Bible all day . . .'

Elizabeth's jaw dropped. 'Missionaries? But I'm sure you said . . .' she began once she had regained control of it.

'. . . and the head missionary, his wife had a viola and she decided to teach me to play. Remember, Elizabeth?' Gloria urged her friend. 'I told you about them. The MISSIONARIES?'

'Oh. Right. Of course! The ones that taught you how to wear clothes?' Elizabeth asked, getting into the spirit of it. The circle of girls around Gloria, Ruth and Elizabeth now included every member of the form. 'And stopped you putting bones through your nose?' she reminded her solemnly.

'That's right,' Gloria nodded. 'If you look right up my nose, Ruth, you can still see the scar. After they took the bone out, it healed right up.'

'Don't you want to get up Gloria's nose, Ruth?' Elizabeth asked, all innocence.

'Oh, we used to sit under the shade of a fever tree . . .' Gloria reminisced.

'On the banks of the great, green, greasy . . .' Elizabeth chimed in.

'. . . Kingston River, and recite the alphabet. I used to think that eL eM eN O Peas were something English people ate for tea.'

'But I saw your mother when you first came to school,' Ruth interjected.

'The missionaries lent her dresses to come with me to England. She's probably back in Jamaica right now running around in her bare feet.' The vision of Mother running anywhere, much less barefooted, threatened to break through Gloria's composure.

'Now, Ruth,' Elizabeth said chidingly, 'don't you feel terrible for being so unkind to Gloria?' A circle of accusing faces all looked towards Ruth who squirmed uncomfortably.

'But she's read all those books . . .' she began.

'They used to make us read for an hour every morning, before we had to go and beat our clothes on the rocks to get them clean,' Gloria embroidered, her voice full of pathos.

'They didn't have soap, you see,' Elizabeth explained sadly. The circle of eyes looked even more accusingly at Ruth.

'It's so much better here in England,' Gloria said, 'where everyone just wears the same clothes over and over again so they don't have to wash hardly at all!'

The snort of laughter that Elizabeth could not repress was drowned in the general scramble for seats as Miss Brock's firm tread was heard approaching along the corridor.

Flushed from a vigorous, if often inaccurate, game of tennis, Gloria bounced along the corridors towards the changing room. She was brought up short by Miss Brock's voice.

'Ah, Gloria. Just the person I wanted to see.'

Several other girls turned to look curiously at Gloria. It was unusual for Miss Brock to speak to any of the girls in the corridor beyond a polite good morning or afternoon, or a gentle admonition about their behaviour or appearance.

'Yes, Miss Brock?'

'There is something that struck me as very odd indeed and I wondered if you might be able to explain it to me,' Miss Brock continued. Aware of the many pairs of ears straining to hear what she was saying, she suggested they walk together towards the gardens. Gloria heard the whispering begin before the door to the quadrangle had closed behind them.

'It is,' Miss Brock said, seating herself on a bench shaded by a bower of honeysuckle, 'concerning the missionary work in Jamaica.'

'Missionaries, Miss Brock?'

'Missionaries, Gloria,' Miss Brock said in a stern voice. 'In fact, I have a close acquaintance who is at this very moment teaching in Jamaica and she's never mentioned the excellent work the missionaries of . . . Half Way Tree, is it? . . . were doing. Now how do you explain that, my dear?'

Gloria looked sheepish. 'I can't explain it, Miss Brock.'

'Unless of course Ruth Green was wrong . . . ?' Miss Brock let her voice trail off, allowed her gaze to roam the many beds of roses that were blooming vigorously in the small garden. There was silence for a few seconds, then Gloria gave a deep and despairing sigh.

'It was what she wanted to hear, Miss Brock. I got tired of explaining myself to everybody, so I just made something up.' Gloria glanced up to see the headmistress's disturbingly direct gaze trained on her face. She felt the tops of her ears go warm.

'You shouldn't take advantage of other people's ignorance, Gloria,' she said.

'I've been here for nearly two years now and people still treat me as some sort of curiosity.' Despite her best efforts to control it, Gloria's voice was full of frustration.

Miss Brock returned to contemplating the garden. 'Do you regret coming to school in England then?' she asked softly.

'At first I did. I hated it at first.' A small smile came to Gloria's lips. 'But now I know what I am going to do with my life, so it isn't so bad. I'm going to be a barrister, Miss Brock. Like you wanted to be.'

Surprise, respect, but finally fear for the young woman who sat beside her in the cool shadow of the bower, her dark hair curled tightly around her ebony face, chased each other across Miss Brock's face.

'Perhaps sixteen is a little young to be making such momentous decisions. Life doesn't always turn out as you plan, my dear. Besides, this is an . . . unusual ambition for a girl. You may be disappointed.'

For the first time Gloria looked Miss Brock straight in the eye.

'I won't let myself be, Miss Brock,' she said with such sincerity, it made the older woman wince at the thought of what she was up against. 'I suppose people like Ruth aren't terribly important, so I shouldn't tease her.'

'Quite,' Miss Brock concurred. 'So I can count on you to put everything right?' She rose from the bench.

'Yes, Miss Brock,' Gloria replied reluctantly. 'Miss Brock?'

'Yes, Gloria?'

'Will I always have to be better than everyone else just to be good enough?'

Miss Brock was glad that the sun was behind her as they walked back towards the school building. It would not do for the other girls to see that she was upset.

CHAPTER FOUR

THE GIRLS OF the Mary Datchelor school orchestra could hear the rustling chatter of the crowd filing into the school auditorium from where they sat, behind the heavy velvet curtain. They look like a flock of doves settling to roost in those white dresses, thought Miss Brock, as she watched them tune their instruments and sort out the sheet-music on their stands. Nervous smiles flitted from face to face. Occupying the right-hand seat of the first row of violas sat Gloria, her awareness of her responsibilities as First Viola writ large across her face. The detail and intricacy of the lace collar on her white dress was emphasized by her dark skin beneath it. She must have felt the headmistress's eyes on her, because she looked up at Miss Brock and gave her a small smile. The orchestra was brought to quietude by a few brisk taps of Miss Donnington's baton. She stepped aside to let Miss Brock address the girls.

'Well, ladies,' Miss Brock said, 'this is it – the Mary Datchelor summer concert for 1938. I just wanted to say how terribly proud I am of each and every one of you. I'm sure you will play like angels tonight – just as I'm sure you'll play like angels when we give our usual performance in Munich in July.' A whispered hurrah rose from the girls. 'It is going to be a wonderful trip and I am looking forward to it tremendously. Now remember, when that curtain goes up, smile as if you are really enjoying yourselves. And remember, I have perfect pitch, so I shall know exactly who plays a wrong note!'

An hour and a half later, the auditorium rang with the

applause of enthusiastic parents and families as the curtain fell.

'One more curtain call, ladies. I think two encores are enough, don't you?' Miss Donnington called over the applause. She nodded to Elizabeth who turned away vigorously at the handle that opened the curtains again. The girls stood, curtsied, smiled; Miss Donnington smiled and made a small bow to where Miss Brock sat in the audience, flanked by approving Guild officials and School Board members. The curtain closed for the final time, the applause died away and was replaced by the sound of movement and excited conversation.

Behind the curtain, the First Violin led the girls in three cheers for Miss Donnington – a traditional appreciation which never failed to bring a huge smile and bright red patches to Miss Donnington's cheeks. All the exuberance of an ordeal overcome, and overcome with honour, began to show so when Miss Brock arrived backstage to congratulate them, Miss Donnington had to get their attention by forcibly banging her baton on the nearest music stand. One of the senior girls brought a large bunch of long-stemmed yellow roses to Miss Brock and she handed one with a few quiet words to each of the girls before they went off to join their families and friends in the auditorium. At Miss Brock's request, Gloria and Ruth stayed behind 'for a word'.

'Have we done something wrong, Miss Brock?' Gloria asked, as the last of the girls disappeared.

'No, no. Absolutely not. You both played very well this evening. Very well.' Miss Brock paused, slowly took off her gloves and stowed them in the small beaded purse she was carrying. Gloria noticed for the first time how it matched exactly the colour of the silk frock the headmistress was wearing. Miss Brock nodded as if she had come to a decision.

'I have been debating with myself what exactly I should do about this problem and I've come to rather a sad conclusion. I'm afraid neither of you will be able to come to Munich with the orchestra.'

'But why?' Gloria cried. 'I don't understand!'

'I do.' Ruth said. She loosened her bow, put her lump of rosin into her violin case and snapped it shut, then took up the case, ready and anxious to depart.

'Ruth, dear . . .' Miss Brock said, taking the case from her gently, '. . . there are things happening in Germany of which every decent person must feel ashamed, but I believe we cannot allow this kind of barbaric behaviour to dictate our lives. The Mary Datchelor orchestra has been to Munich every summer for the last five years. I refuse to let the Nazis stop us this time.'

'It's the troubles, isn't it, Miss Brock?' Ruth challenged.

'Yes, my dear. I'm terribly sorry. I know how disappointed you must be.'

Gloria looked from Ruth's flushed and angry face to Miss Brock's sorrowful one.

'What troubles? Why can't I go to Munich?' she demanded.

'Because they don't want people like us there, Gloria,' Ruth said bitterly.

'I'm afraid I must rejoin my guests in the auditorium. After all, it is the Guild which funds the school so I must go and play the hostess,' Miss Brock said, returning Ruth's violin to her. 'You do understand that this was the only sensible decision. I couldn't risk either one of you being harmed. I'm sure the other girls will tell you all about it when they get back from Munich. It will be as if you were there with us yourselves, I'm sure.' She smiled comfortingly then slipped through the curtain back into the bustling auditorium.

'You're crying!' Ruth accused Gloria.

'I'm not!'

'Yes, you are!'

'So what if I am? I worked just as hard as everyone else – I should be going to Munich. Why can't I go?'

'Because, silly,' Ruth said in her most world-weary voice, 'you are coloured. And I can't go because I am Jewish.'

Gloria realized her mouth was hanging open and she shut it with a snap.

'*Jewish?* But you never said ... I mean, I thought you were ... you don't look ... you look so English!'

Ruth raised a finely arched eyebrow. 'I am English. And I am Jewish.'

'But you never said a word!' Gloria was still flabbergasted.

Ruth gave a small sigh. 'There are lots of people right here in England who don't like Jews, you know. Not everywhere is like dear old Mary Datchelor. Besides, it was all I ever heard about at home, being Jewish and what it meant. I didn't want to hear about it at school, too. Ever since the troubles began in Germany, we've had my uncle and his whole family come to live with us. That's all they ever talk about – the houses, the businesses, the friends left behind in Poland.'

Seeing that Gloria was listening intently to her every word, Ruth decided to continue. 'My uncle says that if Hitler had his way, he'd wipe the Jews off the face of the earth. He believes there is going to be another world war, but my father says Mr Chamberlain will sort it out. They argue about things like that all the time.'

Both girls sat side by side in the middle of a spiky sea of musicstands and stools. Suddenly Gloria began to giggle.

'Does that mean that you and I actually have something in common?' she asked.

Ruth began to laugh. 'Don't tell Elizabeth,' she said. 'She'll be terribly jealous.' And as if driven out of them by the pain of Miss Brock's decision, their laughter grew and grew before it quieted to a heavy silence.

'So if you . . .' Gloria began, 'I mean, you were an outsider too, but you were always so unkind to me.'

'Sometimes I wanted to tell you,' Ruth confessed. 'I wanted to, but I was afraid if I said I was Jewish . . .' She let the words trail into another silence.

'But didn't Miss Brock know?'

'Yes, she did. She said it was my choice to tell or not,' Ruth replied. 'You think I'm a coward, don't you?'

'I don't know,' Gloria answered slowly. 'You see, I can't choose whether or not to tell. I always look like what I am.'

'I loved being in the orchestra. I used to think that nobody cared who was making the music so long as it sounded wonderful,' Ruth said with a wry smile.

'But it's not true, is it? Nothing is the same any more,' Gloria agreed. 'Won't your family be wondering where you are?' she asked.

Ruth shrugged. 'It's Friday night – the beginning of our Sabbath. So there's nobody out there waiting for me either.'

One cold, rainy evening in September, at the beginning of the new term, the school auditorium was crammed to capacity with grim-faced parents and children of all ages. The thrumming of the rain on the roof added to the atmosphere of unease. Groups of small children ran screaming and shouting along the usually decorous corridors of the school. Gloria was towed through the auditorium crowd by a determined Elizabeth.

'You have to come and stand with us, Gloria!' She shouted to be heard above the noise of the crowd. 'You can't stand there all by yourself!'

An unsmiling Miss Brock made her way through the throng to the podium. The crowd grew silent.

'First of all,' she began, 'may I say thank you to you all for coming out in such number on such an inclement evening. As I'm sure you are all aware, the news is not good. Because of the risk of air raids to London, the authorities have decided to close all London schools and declare a state of emergency. When this happens, Mary Datchelor has been asked to organize a school migration for our students and we need your co-operation.'

'You'll have to come and stay with us,' Elizabeth told Gloria confidently. 'There are three of us if you count Jane since she's only six, so I'm sure whoever we have to stay with when we are evacuated can put you up too.'

'Leave London? But how will I ever get home, if I leave here? I don't want to leave London!'

'But you have to. Doesn't she have to, Mummy?' Elizabeth tugged vigorously on her mother's sleeve. 'Tell Gloria she can stay with us, please! She won't listen to me.' Elizabeth's mother smiled sheepishly at Gloria.

'I'm trying to hear what Miss Brock is saying, Elizabeth,' she said. 'Why don't we talk about this when we get home?'

'But Gloria doesn't have any family here so she has to—'

'I said we would talk about it at home, child!' Elizabeth's mother snapped. Gloria set off for the auditorium door, pushing her way through the dense crowd. Elizabeth, alarmed, tried to follow but lost her in the crush.

Outside the front gates, Gloria stopped and dragged the cold, damp autumn air into her lungs. The streetlamps made weak pools of light on the pavement. The whole street seemed desolate, the shadows encroaching. The rain poured down relentlessly, finding its way down the neck of her coat. Hunching her shoulders, she set off to walk back to Mrs Chagler's, driven on by the thought of being able to close her room door behind her and climb under the covers. Then she could wait for her heart to slow, then she could figure out what she was going to do.

Radnor,   *October 27th, 1938*
Half Way Tree Post Office
St Andrew

Dear Gloria,

I felt as if someone had walked over my grave when I read the telegram from Miss Brock. Thank goodness they cancelled the migration in the end, but Father has decided he is not going to have you there one minute longer. I went downtown and organized your passage home that same afternoon and your ticket will be at the shipping office by the time you get this. They promised faithfully that they would deliver it to you right away.

Mrs Marley thinks that this Mr Hitler is on the right track in Germany because she was reading some magazine that said he was giving hope to ordinary people. When you come home, you can tell her what you've heard about him in England. Father says there will be war.

Don't tell Father because he says I shouldn't bother you, but I want you to go and buy him another pair of boots like the ones I got for him. I am sure you remember the shop on Oxford Street where we bought them. The outline is of his right foot so they should be able to size and fit them from that. You know the kind he likes.

I'm saying a prayer for you every day until you get home. Cook has already planned your welcome home dinner and she has her eye on my fattest brown hen. She is hoping the gungo peas will bloom early so she can stew them with pig's-tail for you as well.

It seems like the whole world is in an upset. We have had no end of trouble here, with the stevedores and the sugar-workers striking for better pay. Father says he often sees the houses they live in when he travels around with his work, and he believes they deserve better.

I tell him not to say so too loudly because the Governor is very angry about the whole thing and they have thrown a man called Bustamante in jail. Apparently he stood up between the police and the strikers and pulled open his shirt and offered to let the police shoot him! The newspapers are full of it. Father says something has to change before the riots spread everywhere. Maybe Armageddon really is coming. Reverend Gibson preached a mighty sermon about that this Sunday, but I will tell you all about it when I see you.

Godspeed, Gloria. I won't sleep one night through until you are back home where you belong. Remember to keep your trunk in your cabin and don't store anything in the hold. That way you will know that what left England will arrive in Jamaica!

Mother

P.S. If you see them, please buy me a half dozen linen handkerchiefs. The heat right now is terrible and I use two or three in one day! I can't wait for the Christmas breeze to start blowing!

Standing as far forward as she was allowed on the deck of the banana boat, Gloria spotted Mother and Father long before the ship slid into its moorings alongside Victoria Pier in Kingston Harbour. Dressed as ever in his khaki trousers, white cotton shirt, Panama hat and working boots, Father was standing, legs apart, squinting into the afternoon sun, as sturdy and foursquare as ever. Mother sat, fanning herself, in a huge, black Austin just behind him. Even from a distance, Gloria could see that what had been a sprinkling of grey when Albertha left England had become a streak of white in the thick hair she dressed back from her face. The soft yellow morning suit she was wearing fitted neatly to her tall frame.

In less than half an hour, Gloria was in the back of the Austin, sandwiched between her parents, her trunk and two cases strapped to the sides of the car.

'Isn't it nice?' Mother asked, patting the shiny leather seat. 'The running boards are so wide we can pack enough for a whole weekend in Montego Bay with no trouble at all, can't we, Will?'

'Yes, mi love,' Father concurred, smiling at his daughter.

'It's very nice, Mother,' Gloria agreed.

Mother reached forward and tapped the chauffeur on his shoulder. 'Home, Sibley. And drive the long way. I want everybody to see my daughter is back home.' As they pulled away from the bustle of the docks and drove along King Street where all the largest Kingston shops jostled shoulder to shoulder for the many customers strolling along the wide, tree-lined pavements, Mother turned an appraising look on her daughter.

'You've grown,' she said. 'And you speak very well. And that is a very nice suit.'

'You did say buy the best,' Gloria reminded her.

'Well, now that you are home, everybody wants to see you. And we are going to need your help with the Christmas pageant. No one can figure out a way to make snow that looks like the real thing.'

'You see that our cultural horizons haven't got any wider since you've been gone, child,' Father whispered as Mother ploughed on enthusiastically.

'Father, I need to speak to you and Mother,' Gloria began. They were sitting together on the front verandah, drinking three large glasses of Cook's bellywash – a strong orangeade made with coarse brown sugar and the bitter juice of Seville oranges – and sweating gently in the heat. Father puffed on his pipe. Mother continued reciting the list of activities she had planned for Gloria, interspersing it with anecdotes about the people who populated her world. Gloria, staring across the lawn towards the fence and the street beyond, smiled to see the tram rumble by and noticed that the poinsettias were just beginning to redden. She waited until her mother had paused before speaking.

'I wish Mrs Marley was here right now to hear how nicely you speak,' Mother said proudly, but Father glanced at her and she fell to silence.

'I wanted to tell you that I've decided what I want to do with my life,' Gloria said, surprised how certain she sounded. 'I want to go back to England.'

'But there is going to be a war,' Mother declared, looking to Father for support.

'I have to go back. I want to study law.' The pin-drop silence was eventually broken by the soft, popping sound of Father drawing on his pipe.

'Don't be silly, Gloria. A woman barrister? Never!' Mother said.

'Let the child speak, Mother. Nothin' wrong with having ambition,' Father interrupted.

'Miss Brock said that is what she wanted to be!' Gloria asserted.

'Well then, I am going to write that woman a very strong letter, filling your head full of rubbish,' Mother rejoined. 'My Gloria study law like a man? Throw away the benefits of all that English schooling? Over my dead body, Will Carter, you hear me? Over my dead body!'

CHAPTER FIVE

'GLORIA! WAKE UP child!'

Gloria was aware of the smell of the kerosene lamp before she even opened her eyes to see Father standing at the end of her bed.

'Is something wrong, Father? What time is it?'

'Nothing wrong and it is three-thirty in the morning,' Father whispered. 'I need an able body to help me surveying today. Just remember to be quiet like a mus-mus because we don't want to wake your mother.' He placed the lamp on her dresser before sliding silently from the room.

Puzzled, Gloria dressed as quickly and as quietly as she could. The morning air was cool, laden with the scent of the rain that had poured throughout the night and still gently dripped off the trees, as she joined Father by the Austin under the lignum vitae trees that shaded the driveway where it curved past the verandah. He looked her over in the headlights, nodding with approval at the cotton skirt and blouse, the sturdy shoes and socks she had chosen to wear.

'Does Mother know I am coming with you?' Gloria asked as he steered the Austin out of the gate into the still, dark streets, the hooded headlamps barely illuminating even the narrow strip permitted by the stringent blackout regulations. 'She was planning to take me shopping for material for a new church frock on King Street today.'

'You can't spend the whole summer shopping, child.

45

Besides, I told your mother I was going to take you with me one day.' Father glanced at his daughter mischievously. Gloria did not look mollified. 'I left her a note on the kitchen table, mi love,' he comforted her, relenting. 'After all, a man needs to know that his dinner will be waiting on him after a long day's work.'

Father stood on the driver's seat and peered into the gloom beyond the headlights. As the first green light of dawn streaked the sky behind him, he sized up the muscular flow of the Ferry River as it crossed the road fifteen feet beyond where he had stopped the car. The night's rains had swollen its volume and what had been clear, green water sidling placidly across the St Catherine plain south to the sea was now a khaki-coloured and opaque flow, restlessly probing the bank for weakness, gnawing away and threatening to overwhelm the grassy bank. Father lit his pipe and stared thoughtfully at where the river buried the bridge he needed to cross under swirling waters two feet deep.

As the sky lightened, Gloria looked around her and saw the hunched shoulders of the limestone hills that looked down past where they were parked, across the mangrove-riddled plains, towards the south coast of the island. She could smell the brackish water from the swamps, and remembered uncomfortable stories, gleefully told, of six-foot crocodiles seen in amber pools, of goats and children grabbed and dragged to a twirling, helpless death in among the gnarled roots.

'Damn nuisance,' Father muttered.

'Missa Carter? A you dat, sah?' A man clad only in a sturdy but stained pair of trousers strode out of the shadows towards the Austin, lighting his way with a smoking bottle torch.

'Morning, Miss,' he said to Gloria, tipping an imaginary

cap. 'River vex, Missa Carter,' the man observed philosophic-
ally. He fished a small clay pipe and the remains of a length
of jackass rope tobacco out of his pocket and filled his pipe,
lighting it from his torch. 'Look like you going have to use
old-time people transport today.'

'How much this time, Missa Newton?'

'Where yu going?'

'Back to Francis Lodge Estate. They looking to build a new
house for the overseer.'

'Ah. So you want to cross the river and a dray to take you to
the estate?' the man suggested, suddenly alert, sharp as the
new light that lanced across the sky. Father nodded. 'And a
lad to watch you car till you come? You know I always charge
a fair price, Missa Carter. But times is hard and prices can't
stay the same for ever.' Father turned away from him to size
up the bridge again.

'Ten shillings and I will take you there and back miself. I
have a new young mule, Missa Carter, a lovely little barble
jack dat never get tired. Drive you there miself.' Father still
looked doubtful. 'After all, Missa Carter, you would never
want a nice young lady like this to end up drownded sake of a
few shillings.'

It seemed to Gloria that the flat-bedded ferry tugged
ferociously at the rope that was slung from bank and bank and
on which Mr Newton pulled manfully to guide it across the
swollen river. The battered leather cases containing Father's
surveying equipment, including his precious theodolite, were
secured in the centre of the raft by a fraying sisal rope. On
Father's orders, Gloria perched on top of these and clung on
as desperately as dignity would allow. Mr Newton, silent
except for the occasional grunt as he hauled them hand
over hand to the far shore, displayed muscles as corded
and determined as those Gloria thought she could see in the

water that tried to wrest the raft away from his control. It was
a relief to plant her feet on the muddy grass of the opposite
bank.

Clucking at his precious mule, Mr Newton turned the dray
off the main road to trundle along a dirt road between fields
of cane which stood ten feet high on either side. The leaves,
brilliant in the sparkling morning air and still dappled with
drops of water from the night's rain, were the most intense
green Gloria had ever seen, the dark earth at their feet the
richest brown. They passed knots of schoolchildren, making
their way to school, uniforms immaculately pressed, their
shoes draped around their necks on their laces for fear of the
mud. Father, sitting beside Mr Newton as he drove, seemed
to know them all by name and returned their polite good
mornings with gusto.

'I don't see young Lawrence this morning,' Father
observed to Mr Newton. Once his travails at the ferry had
finished, Mr Newton had produced a much-washed shirt and
flat cap from his pocket and put them on before he took the
reins of the dray. He looked across at Father under the brim of
his cap before replying.

'Terrible t'ing 'bout Missa Lawrence,' he said. 'Hand slip
with the machete out in the field and him get cut bad bad.
Next t'ing you know gangrene take di leg. Doctor seh nutting
to do but cut it off. So you know how that story go. Him was
champion cane-cutter in '35 too. You see how life hard for a
poor man.'

Gloria, riveted by what she heard, looked from Mr
Newton's resigned face to Father's stony features.

'You know where they living?' Father asked.

'The Lawrence family? Should still be somewhere on
the estate, sah. People trying to help dem out, you know.
Throw a little partner for them to put something in dem

pocket. But you know they can't stay long now. Housing is for dem dat work on the estate, dem dat can still cut cane.'

'Find them.'

An hour later, the dray drew up outside one of the row of wooden houses where the cane-cutters and their families lived. Perched on wooden stilts and all built to exactly the same design, the houses seemed to Gloria to be full to bursting of women and children and dogs and cooking and washing. A thin woman stood at the top of the steps and watched as Father climbed down off the dray. She pushed her children behind her into the house, folded her arms over her breasts and stood feet apart, ready to face him. To Gloria watching from the dray, her face seemed as hard and as grey as the rocks around which the Ferry River had swirled. Her clothes hung loose on her thin body.

'We not leaving,' she said. 'We don't have nowhere to go and you don't have no right to throw mi husband away like this . . .'

Before she could continue, her son pushed past her and raced down the steps to shake Father's hand.

'Is Missa Carter, Mama,' he said, his thirteen-year-old voice dancing between a rumble and a squeak despite his best efforts to control it.

'I met your son when I surveyed the land for the factory extension, Mistress Lawrence,' Father explained. 'Helped me fetch and carry. Good boy. Good sensible boy. I was sorry to hear that he wasn't in school.'

Mrs Lawrence's face softened with uncertainty then hardened again. Her anger against the world was a habit she found hard to shake off.

'School is a waste of time for all like him,' she spat. 'Him going have to find work now. Else di whole of wi going to starve.' The boy hung his head in embarrassment. The silence on the sunny, delapidated verandah was palpable.

Out of the darkness of the house, the soft sound of padded crutches and a dragging foot approached.

'She thought you was the bailiff, Mas' Will,' Mr Lawrence said, emerging slowly into the daylight. His shoulders were broad, his remaining leg finely muscled. Where his foot touched the ground, the yellow calloused sole and dusty toes planted themselves like they had been there for ever. He had folded under the end of his empty trouser leg and tucked it neatly into his belt. Despite the flesh that had fallen away from his rangy frame, despite the sudden years that pain had etched on his face, Gloria found it easy to believe that he had been champion cane-cutter of '35.

'Is that the daughter you was telling us about over dat glass of red rum at Myrtle's Tavern last time you was here?' he asked, smiling at Gloria. 'Come inside, miss. Can't travel all this way and leave you sitting out in the hot sun. Manners maketh the man. You too, Missa Newton.'

It wasn't until she sat wearily in the back of the dray as it picked its way back along the dirt road by the light of two smoking bottle lamps that evening, that Gloria realized that the bowl of porridge, sweetened with sugar as dark as molasses and flavoured with the fragrant nutmeg kept in a tightlidded jar on the top shelf of the kitchen cupboard, that she had eaten at the Lawrence family home had probably been cooked as breakfast for the four children who sat and watched her eat it with exquisite politeness.

She felt a burning rush of shame and anger travel through her body at her own ignorance, at her slowness in realizing how different her protected existence was from the lives of people she saw yet did not always notice around her. All day, as she hiked across bushland and held instruments whose names she could barely remember under her father's patient instruction, the sight of the champion cane-cutter of '35, of his son's bright face, of his wife's grey anger, had haunted her. The glimpse she had had of a wood fire fanned to life in the back yard, of a small bedspread with patched sheets and sleeping pallets made of stuffed burlap bags hastily folded out of sight as she entered the house: all these things stayed with her until she felt she could touch and see them by just closing her eyes.

It was not until she sat beside Father as he piloted the Austin back across the plain towards Kingston that she felt she could speak. Father, never a man for words when silence would do, stared along the headlit road alert for dithering chickens and dashing goats, and glanced only occasionally at his daughter.

'Do you think the war will ever end, Father?'

'The question is when, child, not if. Mankind has a terrible talent for needless cruelty but it can't last for ever. Why you ask?'

'What will happen to the Lawrences?'

'I going to have a word with one of the supervisors. I'm sure with a little persuasion they can find him a job driving a cart. Something. A man like that needs to work.'

'And if they won't?'

'Between you, me and this dusty road?' Father asked, swerving generously to avoid a rain-enlarged pot-hole. 'I will make sure they are all right. That lad is too bright not to be in school. But you are not to say a word to your mother.'

'She says you are kind to a fault, that you let people take advantage of you.'

'There but for the grace of God, child. That's why I do it. The grace of God.'

They drove in thoughtful silence for several minutes more. The first scattered houses near Dunrobin told them they would soon be home. Father blew his horn loudly at a dozen swaggering young men who stepped into the darkened roadway in the Austin's path, chatting loudly.

'I'll be glad when this damn war is over and done with so they can let us have some street-lights again,' he muttered darkly.

'What gives the estate-owners the right to treat Mr Lawrence so badly? It makes me so angry that people can be treated like that, can be turned out on the street like that. It's just like when Mrs Chagler thought she could—'

Father glanced across, surprised by his daughter's sudden silence. She was staring ahead of her, eyes full, mouth set. 'You look like your mother when you do that.'

When she finally spoke, Gloria felt the words tumble from her lips with all the force of the flooded Ferry River.

'Let me go back and study. Please, Father. I'm doing my Senior Cambridge in January and all the teachers say I will pass. I know Mother doesn't want me to study law, and I know I said I would forget about it, but please, Father. I have to. I have to try. I have to try and stop things like this from happening. I won't let you down. I promise.' Father drew breath to reply but was not given a chance to utter a word. 'You always said that a good education was more precious than gold and this is all I've ever wanted. I know it's a lot to ask, but—'

'Who is going to tell your mother?'

'You read about it every day in the papers, all the things that women are doing while the men are at war, so why can't I be a lawyer? I know it isn't the same as building airplanes, but—'

'I suppose I could use that as one argument,' Father said as he manoeuvred the Austin through the gates and let it run to a halt down the drive. Gloria stared at him in open-mouthed astonishment as he calmly switched off the ignition and climbed out, stretching luxuriantly and beating the dust of the day off his clothes with his hat. 'You may study, child, but you're not going back to England until the War is over. That is too much to ask.'

Mother, shaded lantern in hand and swathed in one of the voluminous white cotton nightdresses of which she was very fond, appeared at the top of the verandah steps.

'About time the two of you find yourselves home,' she remarked, ushering them up the steps. 'Don't you dare smile at me like that! I don't know what gets into your head where your daughter is concerned sometimes, Will Carter, having the child up hill and down dale like any tomboy.'

She closed the front door behind them. 'And as for you, Gloria Carter, don't you know that you should not be jumping up and down and laughing like a madwoman? That is not what I would call ladylike deportment!'

The hiss of snow under the large wooden skis on which Gloria fought to stay upright filled her ears. Her descent of the nursery slope had begun with a good-natured shove in the back by one of her companions during her first winter in Canada. Now it had become a desperate effort to keep her skis in line and her dignity intact as she slid inexorably down the slope. She struggled for balance within the confines of her heavy winter clothes, feeling the poles slipping away from her mittened fingers.

'Gloria!'

The sound of her own name startled her and she tried to turn and look where the voice had come from. The hissing grew louder, rhythmic, sinister. She could no longer see the snow or feel the weight of the skis on her feet. The sensation now was that of sliding uncontrollably, yet her limbs were too heavy to move.

'For goodness sake, wake up! We have to get moving soon, or else we'll have to sleep outdoors again tonight!'

Gloria's eyes snapped open. Blinking in the late afternoon light, she could still hear the swish of snow under her skis. It stopped. Joan Didier finished pumping up her bicycle tyre, her broad face wreathed in smiles with several of her ringlets pasted to her forehead from the effort.

'The skiing dream again?' Joan asked. Gloria nodded. 'Honestly. You'd think after three winters you'd have forgotten all about the incident.'

'I thought I had,' Gloria shot back, stung.

Joan came to sit beside Gloria. The grand sweep of the St Lawrence lay before them, the sun setting at its own languid summer pace over its waters.

They had talked about taking this trip ever since they met during their first year at Toronto University. Joan, a proud Quebecoise, had felt herself something of an outsider among the shiny moneyed faces at their college. Like Gloria, she had put her head down and worked hard but had made herself less and less popular with the lecturers as the years wore on. She would not, and secretly felt she could not, let anything pass that smacked of privilege and was not afraid to stand up in the middle of a crowded lecture hall and challenge her teachers.

Joan and Gloria had become firm friends over one Easter Holidays. As a foreign student, Gloria had no choice but to stay in the hall of residence. Joan had chosen to do so, worried she was not going to pass her exams if she returned home to the energetic household full of tumbling siblings and vigorous conversations in Montreal. Gloria's presence calmed and chanelled Joan's energy. Joan's friendship allowed Gloria to peer over the walls she lived behind.

They had studied together that holiday and ever since then. They also got into the habit of taking long, rambling walks around the campus and beyond as they revised. Joan would point out even in the middle of the city the ways in which the plants and animals made lives for themselves; the starting of bulbs in spring, the crows' nests revealed by the autumn's leaf fall, the squirrels' frugality.

During one of their long walks they had come to the shores of Lake Ontario. To be near water stirred strong memories of home for Gloria and she found herself suddenly near to tears.

'My mother grew up in the country,' Gloria explained. 'Every summer we would go up into the hills to visit my aunt and uncles, a place called Swift River. There was a swimming hole she took us to. I've never seen water so blue. Rose apple trees grew all along the bank and we'd sit in the sun and eat them then turn over the rocks in the shallows and hunt for crayfish.'

Joan glanced over at her friend. Gloria was looking at the water, wearing, as she frequently did when she talked of home, a half smile. She felt Joan's eyes on her and gave herself a little shake.

'Memories.'

'It sounds wonderful,' Joan assured her. 'In fact, I think we should cycle the St Lawrence seaway this summer just so you can keep your feet wet. It'll take a couple of weeks, but I'm sure you'll enjoy it. The river and the islands all intertwined, so spectacular. And I know the best ways through the fields and the woods, so we can avoid the roads if we want to.'

They hadn't gone that summer, of course. It had taken them three years to save up enough to pay for the expedition, Gloria determined not to go anywhere without a sturdy tent and a nearly new bicycle. Now here they were, graduation safely behind them, sitting on the banks of the St Lawrence in the long rays of the afternoon sun.

'When do you sail for home?' Joan asked. 'I shall start saving again immediately, you know. I am determined to visit Jamaica. As soon as this war is over and it is safe.'

Gloria knew this was the moment she had been waiting for, a moment she had dreaded.

She reached over and unbuckled a small compartment on her rucksack and extracted a letter. She handed it to Joan without comment.

'Cambridge.' Joan said.

'Yes.'

'Cambridge, England.'

'Yes'.

'Across the Atlantic.'

Gloria met Joan's eyes, noted the small worry lines that had appeared over her nose. Joan handed back the letter.

'Well, if you are going to sail the seven seas, we might as well have a really good time before you go,' Joan opined, getting to her feet and dusting herself off. 'Cambridge, eh. *Bon chance, mon amie.* For me, a law degree is enough. But not for you, eh. You must go all the way and become a lawyer at one of the best university in the world in the middle of a war. I should have known you would not do anything the easy way.'

*C*HAPTER SIX

THE SHIP'S LIGHTS bounced off a placid sea under a starless sky. Within the dining room, stewards danced skilfully between the tables, sliding portions of vegetables or slices of roast beef onto the passengers' plates. Gloria, dressed in a simple belted dress in dark green linen, sat at a table with a large, middle-aged Canadian man whose brown suit had deeply offended the thin Englishwoman dressed in a forbidding black taffeta frock who sat opposite him. The clatter of conversation and cutlery made it hard to hear the pianist who sat near the entrance to the dining room, playing an eclectic mix of tunes from 'Tipperary' and 'White Cliffs of Dover' to some Scott Joplin ragtime and the latest melodies by Count Basie.

On the bridge, the even rumble of the engines was broken by a steady blip from the radar screen.

'Damn,' the Captain muttered. 'Cut the engines. Tell the Chief Steward we're going to have to run in silence so he'll have to keep the passengers quiet down there.' A junior officer obediently departed. 'So,' the Captain said, staring out into the blackness, 'now we wait. There hasn't been a U-boat in these waters since '42, but better safe than sorry, eh?'

The stewards passed swiftly from table to table, each one of which fell silent as soon as they finished their whispered announcement, then they drew heavy curtains across each porthole. The engines too fell so silent that the passengers could hear the slap and wash of the waves on the side of the ship, could feel when it slowed and began to wallow. The lights, as glittering as the conversation a few moments before, were dimmed so that the passengers could only just make out the faces of their dinner companions.

'Well, this is one to write home to your family in – where is it, Jamaica? – eh, Miss Carter?' the Canadian man whispered, smiling determinedly. The Englishwoman looked at them both with burning scorn and twisted her lace handkerchief between bony fingers.

'It took me a year to persuade my mother to let me go and study in Canada,' Gloria said, as normally as she could considering her stomach was knotted with fright. 'If I tell her about a brush with a U-boat on my way to study in England, she'd come and fetch me home herself, war or no war.'

'You don't really think it could be a U-boat, do you?' the Englishwoman hissed at the Canadian. 'We're not a military target!'

'Captain is probably thinking better safe than sorry,' he said soothingly. 'It's very unlikely, very unlikely.'

'If they don't start the engines soon, I'm going to get very seasick,' Gloria said, hearing the edge of hysteria in the woman's voice and trying to distract her.

'It's the rolling that does it. When it pitches, it ain't so bad, but the rolling will get you every time,' the Canadian agreed.

'Shouldn't they be issuing us with life-jackets by now?' the woman demanded, her handkerchief a tiny, twisted ball between her fingers. 'Shouldn't they know by now if it is a U-boat?'

'It's probably a good sign that they aren't,' Gloria whispered, watching the fine lace of the handkerchief coming apart under her tearing fingers. The silence was as heavy and smothering as wet wool.

'Whatever it is you're going to study in England must be mighty important to you, Miss Carter, to risk all this,' the Canadian said to Gloria.

'I'm going to get my LLB – my Bachelor of Laws,' Gloria replied. 'I did my first degree at the University of Toronto.' The Canadian smiled and nodded blankly. 'Once I get my LLB and pass my Bar exam, they'll call me to the Bar at one of the Inns of Court and that's it: I'll finally be a lawyer,' Gloria explained.

'A lawyer! And where are you going to be studying all this?' he asked.

'Cambridge.' The woman's eyes focused sharply on Gloria as she continued. 'I've been offered a place at Girton College. Term starts in two months.'

'Cambridge? *You?* And they know you are coloured?' she snapped, her terror forgotten.

'They know my marks are good enough!' Gloria replied equally tartly.

Just as the Canadian opened his mouth to say something conciliatory, the engines rumbled once, twice, then roared into full, pulsing life. Someone applauded, several people laughed with relief. The piano-player struck up another tune.

'Cambridge, eh?' The Canadian man grinned at Gloria, deliberately ignoring an indignant snort from their table companion. 'From what I hear, it's a wonderful place. You'll be living very nicely there, young lady. Very nicely indeed.'

'And this,' Miss Norman said, throwing wide the heavy wooden door, 'is your room, Gloria.' She was the sort of woman who, being of average height and average build and with brown hair peppered with grey, might seem ordinary except for a certain confidence in her carriage, a certain humour around the eyes. Her clothes, like those of so many women Gloria had seen since arriving in wartime England, were utilitarian. Her hands were strong.

'I know the wallpaper bears an unhappy resemblance to stale oatmeal, but décor has hardly been a wartime priority,' she commented, hauling back the heavy curtain to reveal an arched window and the view of the college grounds beyond in all their September glory. 'The portress will bring your trunks along as soon as they are delivered from the station.' Miss Norman came to stand beside Gloria as she stood looking out of the window. 'Leeks,' she explained. 'Leeks and potatoes. We find they grow best here. No more rolling lawns, I'm afraid. And we do have to share the building with fire-watchers and nurses on rest leave from London, so there isn't much in the way of peace and quiet.'

'Yes, Miss Norman.'

'The menu includes whale, horse and I'm ashamed to say, the odd swan,' the woman continued briskly. 'All edible, if not exactly delicious. We grow most of our own vegetables but anything sweet it is "to each their own", I'm afraid. We tried pooling our coupons once but the squabbling in Hall over the jam simply got worse and worse, so we decided against it.' She smiled at the look of astonishment on Gloria's face. 'Oh, food is a matter of great importance now, my dear. If you have a spare moment, it might be edifying to read the comments in the book we keep in Hall on the best way to prepare pickled beetroot. We are, I'm afraid, divided into those who believe that vinegar should be applied when the beetroots are warm, and those who are passionately certain that it should only be added at the table!'

'I see,' Gloria replied.

'You look a little overwhelmed,' Miss Norman remarked as

she made for the door. 'Is there anything else you need to know?'

Gloria looked around the drab room in dismay, at the bucket of coal lying by the small brazier, at the huge, black curtains, the sturdy desk and chair.

'No, Miss Norman,' she said. 'I'll be fine. I suppose I hadn't realized how much things had changed since I was here before the war. It makes five years seem like a very long time.'

'A different world, I'm afraid,' Miss Norman agreed. 'That bucket of coal is your ration for the week and each student is responsible for drawing the blackout curtains in their room. Oh, and make sure that crack in the window is always stuffed with newspaper. They say the winds blow across the fens to Cambridge directly from Siberia.'

'Where can I buy a bicycle, Miss Norman? I think I am going to need one. I hadn't realized Girton was so far away from the Law Faculty.'

'Speak to the portress when she brings your trunks over. If there's one to be bought, she'll know about it. Right,' Miss Norman said, her task complete, 'remember you are expected at tea with the Mistress at four. Oh, and there is a package for you at the Porter's Lodge.'

'That'll be from my mother,' Gloria explained, smiling broadly for the first time since her arrival. 'She thinks I'm going to starve to death so she sends me regular care packages.'

'An eminently sensible woman,' Miss Norman said approvingly. She took one last look around the room. 'Well, Gloria,' she continued, opening the door and revealing a glimpse of the long corridor beyond. The worn carpet was lifting in sinuous waves in the draught that whistled along it. 'I hope you know how tremendously fortunate you are to be here at Cambridge – and at Girton!'

Radnor　　　　　　　　　　　　　　　　　*July 10th, 1944*
Half Way Tree Post Office
St Andrew

Dear Gloria,

If you are reading this it means you are safe and well in England. As soon as you finish reading it, put pen to paper immediately and write me! Please put aside the Christmas cake until Christmastime. I know how much you like it. I have already put a good amount of rum on it so all you have to do is keep the tin closed until Christmas. Cook insisted on sending the guava cheese and coconut cake for you: she still thinks you are the eighteen-year-old who left to go to Canada. She won't believe me that now you are a young lady, you are not interested in sweeties: she even bought paradise plums and jujups to send, too!

How do you find England? Is it very different from when I was there with you? I think very fondly of my days in London. I was telling Mrs Marley so just the other day. She hasn't made it to England yet. She was saying how nice it must be to get away from all the heat in the tropics. I wonder what she would have to say for herself after a night or two shivering in Mrs Chagler's Boarding House for Ladies. Has the Blitz really damaged all those beautiful old buildings?

Can you imagine? Mrs Marley managed to get her picture in the Daily Gleaner *riding her bicycle along King Street as if she was the only one contributing to the war effort. As if all of us aren't doing our best to make do with green banana flour and salt kind. Don't worry, I used my last wheatflour for your cake: banana flour never rises!*

Father has had to park the Austin because of the petrol rationing and now he uses the old buggy he used to use before you were born with two of the most stubborn mules in Christendom when he goes out surveying. Those mules are very smelly and I have had to pull up my rose bushes in the back garden to accommodate them. Even that yellow tea rose I loved so much!

Our first lot of prisoners of war arrived from England a few weeks ago. Italians mostly. The Governor put them to work building barracks up in Hope Valley near Papine. I hear people go and spend hours just looking at them. They've never seen Europeans doing manual labour before! Mark my words, there will be a crop of mulatto babies in that area by next summer. You know how much Jamaicans love to put milk in the coffee!

Look out for doodlebugs and incendiaries and soldiers home on leave. Father sends his greetings. He is fine, working hard as always, and will not give up those boots you brought from England for him in '38. I have had to get the cobbler to resole them twice! No wonder he gets on so well with those mules!

Hermione, Mrs Marley's eldest (plump with puss eyes: I'm sure you remember her), announced her engagement last week and my dear, although Cambridge is famous, it just doesn't compare with a wedding! Such a botheration and you know Mrs Marley: if wedding was an egg, she has to be in the red! Mrs Marley says you are becoming a Blue Stocking, whatever that is. You aren't, are you? I still don't know how you persuaded Father to pay for all this. When I said I wanted you to get a proper education, this was not exactly what I meant. Men don't marry women who know more than they do!

Mother

P.S. You asked for information about the court cases that are in the news here. I enclose some cuttings from the Daily Gleaner. *Mostly people chopping up one another with machetes, or praedial larceny, I'm afraid. Very common.*

P.P.S. Rev. and Mrs Thompson wrote to say that their nephew Garth is staying with them in Southampton, recuperating from a war injury. He sounds like a very nice young man. Mrs Thompson says you are welcome to visit whenever you like. I wrote and said the Christmas vacation would be fine, if the trains are running. It will be just like when you were at school.

★ ★ ★ ★ ★

Gloria created a space in the bed warm enough in which to actually get some sleep by folding the blanket in half, laying her coat over it and then curling up and keeping very still in the cocoon. She felt as if she had only just managed to doze off when a loud banging on her door woke her.

'Yes?' she called sleepily from the shelter of her space. 'Is something wrong?'

'Time to go!' called an improbably cheerful voice from the other side of the door. 'Up and at 'em!'

Tiptoeing across the cold floor, Gloria opened her room door and peered through the dawn gloom at the young woman standing outside.

'Go? Go where?' she asked, shivering in the blast of cold air coming through the door.

'Land work. Everyone has to go, every Saturday. Miss Norman must have told you,' the young woman said, pushing open Gloria's door. Crossing to the window, she pulled back the blackout curtain to let more watery light into the room. Gloria tiptoed back towards her bed.

'I'm Margaret – second-year English, two doors down. Come on, the charabanc is ready to go!' And she steered a reluctant Gloria towards her wardrobe.

'What time is it?' Gloria yawned.

'Six-thirty,' Margaret replied, looking through Gloria's clothes. 'You better get dressed. The driver doesn't like to be kept waiting.'

'Right.' Gloria was trying to rub the sleep from her eyes. 'Dressed. I just need two minutes.'

'What lovely dresses – pleats, gathered sleeves . . .' Margaret pulled down one in a large rose print. 'Ooh, cut on the bias. It's almost sinful!' she breathed.

'Will this do?' Gloria asked, holding up her sturdiest wool

skirt. Margaret looked sceptical. 'Or these?' Gloria showed her a pair of brown lace-up shoes.

'Don't you have any working clothes? Plus you'll need gloves and boots. That outfit won't do at all. You won't last an hour in that.'

'I'm afraid it's all I've got,' Gloria apologized.

'Come on then. Quickly,' Margaret ordered, taking Gloria by the hand. 'My room. I'll lend you something.' Fixing her hair with one hand and grabbing at her warmest jacket with the other, Gloria followed Margaret out of her room. 'The sooner we get there, the earlier we get home – and there's a dance at the Corn Exchange we all want to go to this evening,' Margaret explained.

'My knees hurt, my back aches, my fingers are numb and my feet are on fire,' Gloria groaned as she clambered into the charabanc at the end of the day's work. Margaret leapt nimbly in and settled herself beside her. She looked as if she had been out for a day in the country, hair held neatly in place by a scarf, her overalls almost spotless despite hours of toil. Gloria felt it would be easy to hate her.

'Oh, it was an easy day today, picking apples, wasn't it, girls?' Margaret said cheerfully. There was a chorus of assent from the other occupants of the charabanc. 'Wait till you have to spend the day picking sprouts or scrubbing down pigsties.'

Every jolt of the wagon sent a line of fire up Gloria's spine. Her feet felt so swollen in the heavy leather boots Margaret had lent her, she doubted she would ever get them off. As evening drew down, it began to get colder.

Several of the girls began a hearty chorus of 'Oh Jemima'. Gloria examined her hands for damage to the nails she had worked so hard to grow, and for blisters. She found four.

'Everyone has to do their bit,' Margaret said.

'I know, I know,' Gloria agreed ruefully. 'It's the war.'

'I think you'll make a very good landgirl when you get the hang of it. Besides, there's the dance tonight!'

'I can't stand up straight,' Gloria protested. 'I certainly won't be able to dance. You can tell me how much you enjoyed it tomorrow.'

'Oh, please come. If I'm talking to you, they won't ask me to dance,' Margaret begged.

'In case they might have to ask *me* to dance, too?' Gloria asked gently.

The other girl flushed scarlet to the roots of her hair. 'Well, there won't be any coloured men there and . . .'

'So you just want me to be around and look offputting, rather like a barrage balloon?' Gloria had never seen anyone turn so red.

'No, of course not. Well, yes . . . but I just meant that there will be lots of lovely pilots there and if I am talking to someone, they won't buzz around so much. Can I take my foot out of my mouth now please?'

Gloria couldn't help smiling at her distress. 'Why shouldn't they buzz around?' she asked.

'My Jimmy is in France,' Margaret said proudly. 'We're going to be married when the war's over. He wouldn't mind if I went to the dance, he just wouldn't want me to – you know . . .'

'Fall in love with some dashing pilot.'

'Exactly,' Margaret beamed. 'Please come.'

'I'll think about it.' Gloria tried to squirm into a more comfortable position on the hard wooden seat but gave it up as impossible. Margaret watched her in some amusement.

'I'll let you have my four inches of hot water if you do,' she offered.

'Water isn't rationed too, is it?' Gloria sighed.

'Of course not. Just hot water. So you'll come?'

'I'll think about it. Dances are not exactly the reason I came all this way, you know,' Gloria said quellingly.

'You can't spend your whole time at Cambridge with your nose stuck in some book!' Margaret looked shocked. At that moment the charabanc turned into the gates of Girton and proceeded at a stately pace up the drive, past the huge chestnut trees and through the red brick archway that led to the inner court. In the gathering dusk, the open doors leading to the dining hall were like beacons to shipwrecked and starving sailors. The students piled off the charabanc with renewed energy as it drew to a halt.

'My mother says men don't like bookish girls,' Margaret pointed out to Gloria as they climbed down.

'So does mine,' Gloria said, stretching her aching back. 'But I don't care what men like. I'm here to get my LLB.'

'I still think you should come,' her new friend persisted. 'You might even enjoy yourself.'

'You don't give up, do you?'

Margaret grinned, and slipped her arm through Gloria's so that they could walk side by side.

'And don't you think I would look wonderful in that dress with the pink roses?' she asked innocently.

'*My* dress with the pink roses?'

'Just a thought,' Margaret demurred.

'If you wore that, you wouldn't need a barrage balloon, you'd need an anti-aircraft gun to keep the pilots away!' Gloria opined, grateful to glimpse at the opposite end of the corridor the door to her own room – a room whose lumpy bed now seemed to Gloria to be the last word in creature comforts.

CHAPTER SEVEN

THE LECTURE HALL in the Law Faculty on Trinity Lane was smaller than Gloria expected, the semi-circular banks of wooden seats steeply raked towards the high ceiling. She had just laid out her notebook and pen on the table in front of her when, among the babble of predominantly public-school and English accents around her, she heard another quite distinct voice. It came from a tall young man of Indian appearance who wore with considerable flourish a mustard-coloured waistcoat and a matching flat cap. He was bearing down on her, smiling broadly.

'You wouldn't know how good it is to see another West Indian in the Faculty,' he said. 'The drums told me you were around. Lionel,' he continued, shaking Gloria's hand briskly. 'Lionel Ramkissoon. Guyanese.'

'Gloria . . .'

'Gloria Carter – I know. Your reputation precedes you, my good woman,' he said, imitating the public-school tones of his classmates with uncanny accuracy. 'Jamaican. University of Toronto, right? Henry Mutto was here last year. He graduated the year ahead of you in Canada.' Gloria opened her mouth to say she remembered Henry, but Lionel continued before she could get a syllable out: 'Told us you were coming. He went off and joined up after his first year, foolish boy.'

'Us?' Gloria asked, curious.

'Oh, all the West Indian students from both here and the London School of Economics meet informally every now and then. LSE men were evacuated to Cambridge, you see. Very

convenient, really. We sit around, plot revolutio
each other who we really are. Brought any cigaret
you?' Lionel asked, all in the same breath. Gloria,
words, shook her head. 'Ended up trying to light co
other night, man. Absolutely foul. I might have to
smoking altogether.'

'You did your first degree here?' Gloria asked.

'Yes, man. Came up in '41.' He gave Gloria a smile of
most extraordinary charm. 'Too cowardly to sail home, to
flatfooted to join up, so I thought I might as well study. Pate
doesn't seem to mind paying for it.'

'Don't you want to be a lawyer?' Gloria asked, surprised at
the ease with which they had fallen into conversation.

'Me?' Lionel leaned back expansively, tucking his thumbs
into his waistcoat. 'I used to dream of making my fortune
panning for gold: living rough upcountry as a pork-knocker
like all the other dreamers and vagabonds. Lionel, King of the
Essequibo River.'

'And what happened?'

'Oh, my father had already done it, man. So I thought as a
good son, it was my duty to help him spend his ill-gotten gains.'

'Nice story,' Gloria approved. 'Very romantic. Do all the
girls fall for it?'

For a moment, Lionel's face fell, then he took a closer look
at Gloria and began to chuckle.

'Most of them,' he admitted.

'I know how hard it is to get into this university. I'm sure
you had to work even harder to stay here.'

'Intelligent and perceptive: dangerous qualities in a
woman,' Lionel said, leaning even closer. Gloria managed to
keep a straight face but couldn't hide the twinkle of amusement in her eyes.

'Do you flirt *all* the time?' she asked. Again she was
rewarded with that chuckle.

· dear.'

g beyond Lionel towards the
· one of us.' Lionel turned
· a few seconds. Large,
like a Benin bronze,
ـense of self-consequence

ـnel informed Gloria. 'Wisdom
ـom Nigeria, I think. Has more money
ـnan. Plays on their rugger second fifteen.
ـthe same year. That's all I've heard.'

ـan you've never spoken to him?' she asked,
ـed.

Never,' Lionel confirmed. 'Ah, lecturer coming into view. Must return to my accustomed seat near the door. Best seat in the house. Delighted to have met you, Gloria.'

'You too.'

'This lecturer is a real old windbag but it's all in his latest book so at least I don't have to take notes. I just come to be seen. That's the trouble with us darkies, my dear. We can't hide even in a crowded room.'

By the Spring of the following year, Gloria had learned that by lighting the daily portion of her coal ration in the morning and letting it heat the room for a few hours, she could survive the rest of the day if she sat at her desk in her coat with a horse blanket wrapped round her shoulders. She had decided that it was the dampness of English winters that chilled her to the bone, rather than the cold. She had withstood three Canadian winters, after all. It was the dampness and the gloom, and even the crocuses and signs of buds on the trees did not lift her spirits. She crouched over her desk and forced herself to read. The words were just beginning to fall into place in her head when she was interrupted by a soft knock on the door.

'It's open.'

'May I come in?' Margaret asked, poking her head around the door.

'I have to hand this essay in tomorrow morning.' Gloria did not look up as she spoke.

'Of course,' Margaret said, backing out of the room. 'I'm sorry.' Gloria looked up, her attention caught by a note in her friend's voice.

'Is everything all right, Margaret?'

'I'm fine. Fine. You get on with it,' Margaret insisted. Gloria looked back down at her work, expecting to hear the door shut. 'It's just that I haven't heard from Jimmy for nearly two weeks now.' Gloria glanced up with a little frown. 'It's happened before, of course it has. I'll probably get a letter tomorrow. I'm fine. Absolutely.'

This time the door did close behind Margaret. Gloria tried to settle back into her reading, then gave a deep sigh.

'Not very charitable, Gloria,' she muttered to herself. She stood, shrugging off the blanket, and went to the door and opened it. 'Oh!'

'Try to contain your joy, my good woman,' Lionel Ramkissoon urged as he breezed past her into the room, looking around him with curiosity.

'I was hoping to catch Margaret,' Gloria explained, peering up and down the corridor. 'I think I may have offended her. What on earth are you doing here?'

'Is that how you greet me after I just cycled all the way out from town?' Lionel asked, wounded. 'The sap was rising, Gloria. Spring was in the air!'

'Fool!' She couldn't help chuckling. 'You might as well sit down. Margaret seems to have eluded me.' Lionel threw his rangy frame into Gloria's only armchair, grimacing as he saw the piles of open books on her desk.

'Now I know why Girton is so far out of town. A man

would have to be as fit as a fiddle to get up to any mischief after battling his way up Castle Hill. The mystery,' he said, ' of why Girton girls have such mighty calves is explained.'

'The door has to stay open, I'm afraid. Miss Norman keeps a sharp eye out for these things. May I take your coat?' Gloria asked.

'Not in this room. That's a force-ten draught you have whipping through the place. Any chance of a nip of something to warm the bones?'

'Sorry, the only thing I have with rum in it is the remains of my mother's latest fruit cake.'

'Fetch it out then, my good woman. Didn't your mother ever tell you that the way to a man's heart is through his stomach?' Lionel urged, sliding back into his best public-school tones.

'Is that why you're here? Something to do with your heart?' Gloria enquired in sceptical tones.

'You see? That's what I don't like about a West Indian woman. No trust. She always think a man is after something,' Lionel defended himself, suddenly sounding totally Guyanese.

'And you're not?' Gloria pressed her advantage.

'You see, the thing is, a man has certain needs in this life . . .' Lionel began.

Gloria went and stood by the door. 'Out,' she said.

'No, not like that. I just mean there are certain things a woman can do for a man much better than he can do them for himself.' Gloria raised an eyebrow. 'Especially if he lives in digs,' Lionel continued.

'I mean it, Lionel. I don't have time for this. I have work to do.'

'Not even as a gesture of solidarity for a fellow West Indian?' Lionel pleaded. 'You are a hard-hearted woman, Gloria Carter.'

'Just out of interest: which one was it?' Gloria asked. 'Mending? Or washing?'

Lionel shook his head sadly. 'Now who said anything about mending?'

'I spent three years on campus in Canada, remember? There isn't a trick you lot can pull that I haven't seen. One of my closest friends rubbed her knuckles raw washing her Trinidadian boyfriend's clothes for two years. As soon as he graduated, he married the first pretty blonde that would have him.'

'And you think that I—'

'You won't get the chance, Lionel.'

There was no doubting the finality in her voice. Lionel shrugged, rose from the armchair and, producing a pair of bicycle clips, neatly folded his trousers and fastened them on.

'Do you know how heavy that heap of clothes is? A man could collapse with exhaustion riding all the way back to town with it,' he grumbled.

'Think what wonders it will do for those gangly legs of yours,' she rejoined.

'You are a hard woman.'

'I've had to fight to get here, Lionel. I don't intend to waste any time while I am here. My last Greek lesson was six years ago so I'm way behind.' At the door, Lionel made one last effort.

'Any chance of a slice of that cake? Fortify me for the ride back into town?'

'It's downhill.'

Almost as soon as the door closed behind Lionel, there was a knock on it. Gloria got up and opened it to see Lionel, scarf wrapped around his neck and clutching his bicycle pump, standing there looking worried.

'Yes?' she said patiently. 'What is it this time?'

'Friends?' he asked.

'Absolutely!' Gloria replied, breaking into a wide smile. Relief flooded Lionel's face. As he made his way down the corridor, Gloria heard him singing a cheerful calypso with distinctly racy lyrics, tapping on the wall with his bicycle pump to supply the rhythm.

Gloria caught up with Margaret in the courtyard two days later. The other girl was wheeling her bicycle towards the arched passage that led to the main drive.

'Margaret, wait!' Gloria called, trotting after her. She had spotted her leaving through her room window and had dashed in hot pursuit, wearing only her slippers – a decision she was beginning to regret.

'Finally surfaced from your books, have you?' Margaret asked, wheeling her bike over the damp, crunching gravel. 'I'm heading into town. Need anything?'

'No, no. I'm fine,' Gloria said, her slippers growing more and more sodden as she walked beside her.

'You always say that, Gloria. All work and no play, remember?'

'That's what I came here for, remember?' Gloria countered.

'I've been sitting in my room looking at the walls for hours. I had to get out!' There was no mistaking the edge in Margaret's voice. She was staring determinedly towards the end of the drive as she spoke.

'You still haven't heard from Jimmy,' Gloria said. Margaret glanced across at her, her lopsided smile at odds with the tears standing out in the corners of her eyes.

'You always know when I'm worried, don't you? You're supposed to be fooled by my determinedly gay exterior, Gloria. I work very hard to be charming and vivacious. Oh, don't look so worried. I have heard from Jimmy. He seems all right. Still telling me to study hard, still insisting that he doesn't even look at any of the French mademoiselles.'

'So why is being vivacious such hard work then?'

'Because something is different,' Margaret said, pushing her fingers roughly through her hair, disordering the neat waves into which she had styled it. Gloria noticed that her nails were bitten to the quick. 'He was too guarded, too careful in what he said.'

'Aren't his letters always a bit like that?' Gloria asked gently.

'Oh, I know he never writes scads of pages or anything, but he does try to give me a picture of his life. He knows it makes me feel less frightened if he does that. It's silly, isn't it? They are just words on a page in the end. Just words.' Margaret fought for composure. 'It's just that I couldn't bear the thought of losing him.' The words hung in the air like acrid smoke.

'Maybe he couldn't say more,' Gloria suggested.

'Maybe,' Margaret said. She took a deep breath then began trying to put her hair back in place, her long fingers moving skilfully this time. 'Do you think they really are mustering for one big push?'

'That's what everybody is saying,' Gloria replied, relieved that her friend seemed calmer, more in control. Margaret twisted the last stray tendril into place.

'Please, Gloria, come with me to the concert this evening at King's College Chapel. If I sit around in that room and think any more I shall start climbing the walls.'

'I'm sorry, old thing, I can't.' A vision of her laden desk had flashed before her eyes, and she was feeling the urge to get back to it.

'You're not going to fail if you relax for one evening, you know. You'd think your life depended on getting this degree of yours,' Margaret continued persuasively.

'In some ways, it does,' Gloria replied.

'Rubbish. You're "an handsome lass" as my father used to say. I'm sure there must be some dashing young West Indian dying to sweep you off your feet—'

'I leave all that true love and romance business to you, dear,' Gloria snapped, then continued apologetically. 'It has never been my strong suit, I'm afraid. I'm too blunt for my own good. I've never learnt the art of flattering men.'

'You don't have to sound quite so dismissive, you know,' Margaret teased. 'Men can be really quite nice. You just have your heart set on being a lawyer and you don't want anything to distract you.'

'Touché,' Gloria agreed. 'Actually it started out as a wonderful way to annoy my mother, but I have to admit that getting this far has given me all sorts of delusions of grandeur. I'm beginning to think I might even be able to change a few things – and there are lots of things that need changing at home in Jamaica.'

'I have a soapbox in my room you could stand on, if you like,' Margaret offered. Gloria looked sheepish. Margaret, grinning to see her friend, usually so reserved, speaking so passionately, hopped onto her bike. 'I hope it's enough,' she said, as she cycled away, her tyres crunching on the gravel.

It will be, Gloria thought to herself, watching her go. It has to be enough. Suddenly aware of her cold, damp slippers, she turned back and headed for her room, thoughts of precedence and torts already beginning to churn in her head.

CHAPTER EIGHT

Radnor   *April 11th, 1945*
Half Way Tree Post Office
St Andrew

Dear Gloria,

Mrs Thompson is an old family friend and you have caused me no end of embarrassment with her. I know you got my letter about the Christmas visit because you wrote thanking me for the guava cheese I sent you in the same parcel. Yet you didn't even have the manners to write to Mrs Thompson and let her know you were not going? Shame on you.

I suppose you are so caught up with your new life at Cambridge that nothing else matters to you. I told your father that that is what would happen if he let you go to England. Mrs Marley agrees with me that girls who are too educated are not usually popular. Her daughter's wedding was very beautiful.

There was a heavy storm along the North Coast last week and Father's banana estate near Orocabessa was very badly blown about. Most of the trees are down and even next crop's suckers were damaged. This is by way of explaining why we will not be able to send you your allowance as usual. We will send what we can as soon as possible.

At least Mr Churchill has Hitler on the run. Perhaps life will return to normal soon. I long for such simple things as a slice of bread: there are rumours that we should be getting some Canadian flour soon. When it comes, I'll bake and make up a parcel for you. I'm glad the eggs got there without turning bad: it was Mrs Marley who said to pack them in salt but I wasn't sure it was going to work!

Please write and apologize to Mrs Thompson. You've missed your chance with her nephew anyway. Apparently, he has decided to marry one of his nurses!

Mother

P.S. *In answer to your question, the most successful law firm in Jamaica is Bernard, Ashenheim & Jones. Their chambers are at 32 Duke Street, Kingston. Father met Mr Ashenheim when he went to get his award for services to his profession from the Governor at Kings House. When we get the photographs of the presentation back, I'll send one to you. I ordered an extra one especially for you.*

Gloria looked up from rereading her letter to find that the lecture was almost over, the lecturer gathering his papers with great sweeps of his gowned arms like a benevolent magpie.

'Next week, Miss Carter and Mr Ramsay will make their presentations on the applicability of British family law in colonial societies and I expect it will be as controversial as it usually is,' he said. 'I look forward to a lively debate thereafter. We start promptly at ten. If you arrive at two minutes past, may I suggest you find some other way of passing that hour?' He strode out of the room, closely followed by several of his students, anxious to ask him questions.

Gloria walked away from the Faculty, her head full of thoughts about her parents. So vividly did she imagine her father standing in the middle of the flattened banana walk surveying the devastation of his investment, that she was unaware of the world around her until she felt a sharp tug on her sleeve.

'Hang on a minute!'
'What is it, Lionel?'

'Some of the West Indian students from the LSE are coming over this evening. Wondered if you'd like to join us?'

'I don't think so, Lionel. Some other time.' A spring shower began to drip from a chalky sky and Gloria turned up her collar against it as she walked away. After a moment's hesitation, Lionel caught up with her again.

'You look like death, man. What on earth is wrong?' he demanded, standing squarely in front of her, blocking her progress down the narrow path.

'I'm fine.'

'Like hell you are!' Gloria tried to step around him, but Lionel would not let her. Instead he took her books out of her arms and slipped his free arm through hers. 'You are coming to lunch with me,' he said.

'I said I'm OK,' Gloria insisted, dragged unwillingly along. 'I don't want to go to lunch.'

'Very well,' Lionel said, stopping abruptly, forcing the stream of students behind them to divert around them. 'We can sit on the Backs and wait for the sun to come out, or we could lean over a bridge and grab any punt-poles that pass by. I could even run home and fetch my boater. What do you say to that?'

'You're not going to leave me alone, are you?' Gloria said resignedly.

'Absolutely not,' he concurred, and set off at a brisk pace towards the Backs, towing Gloria behind him. By the time they got there, the shower was over and the river was bathed in spring sunshine that poured from the patches of blue in the sky. Daffodils nodded along the banks. A young man, dressed in a Home Guard uniform, perched on the railing outside Kings College and played a small fiddle, eyes shut, lost in the complexity of his melody.

Lionel spread his jacket on the damp grass and insisted Gloria sit on it.

'Right, pocket battleship. Fire away!'

'I wish you wouldn't call me that!' Gloria protested.

'It is a great compliment, my dear – a tribute to your tenacity and your ability to fight for what you believe in.'

Gloria gave him a scathing look. 'I'm thinking of giving it all up,' she said. 'Going home.'

'Rubbish.'

'If you're not going to listen to what I have to say . . .' she rejoined.

'You're tired, that's all. You feel as though you are standing alone against the world. You think you'll never be able to do anything well enough to please your tutor, your supervisor and more importantly, yourself,' Lionel stated.

Gloria shrugged. 'Is it that obvious?'

'My dear girl!' Lionel replied in his best Etonian accent. 'Rampant perfectionism. Recognized the disease the first time I saw it. Well-advanced, too. Probably pathological. Never suffered from it myself,' he added hastily and smiled, returning to his normal tones. 'Too damn lazy, man.'

'Fool!' Gloria found she was laughing despite herself. They both fell silent, listening to the soaring violin. She glanced across at Lionel and found he was staring into the murky waters of the Cam.

'It's not just that,' she said.

'Aha!' Lionel declared gleefully. 'Now we get to the interesting part.'

'Not interesting, I'm afraid,' Gloria said quietly, aware that several pairs of eyes were now observing them. 'There's nothing interesting to tell. I go to lectures, I go back to my room, I go to Hall, I go to the library. That is the entirety of my life.'

'And whose fault is that?'

'I can't afford to fail, Lionel.' He lay back on the grass, staring up at the sky.

'You are not in the slightest danger of failing. Your tutors may not like the fact that you think British laws are no longer relevant in the West Indies, but they respect the way you say it, pocket battleship!'

He squinted at her, sunlight in his eyes. 'Come on, ducks, tell Lionel all. I know there is more to this.' He waited while she paused.

'Father . . . has had to cut my allowance. In fact, I haven't had anything from him since the end of February. I can make it stretch until the end of term, but . . .'

Lionel sat up. 'Temporarily curtailed or permanently reduced?' he asked briskly.

'I don't know. Mother would never admit things were anything but hopeful but I know they must be pretty bad for him to cut my allowance.'

'May I help?'

Surprised, Gloria looked across at him. 'Absolutely not!'

'I thought you might say that.' After a thoughtful silence, he pointed to one of the mallards paddling along at the edge of the river. 'Just like you,' he said, half-joking. 'Fine plumage. Gliding along. Just gliding along. Nobody knows how hard you are paddling underneath just to keep going.' The gentleness in his voice completely overwhelmed Gloria.

'I just feel so very . . . alone,' she whispered. 'If I want to stay, it looks as though I have to find a way to do it myself. I don't know if I am strong enough any more. I don't know if I have the right to ask my parents to do all this any more.'

'So why did you come here in the first place?'

'You know why I came here. Because I want to be a lawyer. It's all I've dreamed of – for what? Nearly ten years!'

'And you are one year away from realizing that dream!' Lionel insisted.

'In the middle of a war,' she wailed. 'When I am not freezing, I am hungry for a decent meal. I am about to be as

81

poor as a church mouse and am currently top of my tutor's blacklist . . . and always an outsider!' Frustration made her voice sharp.

'We all are, my dear,' Lionel reminded her.

'No,' she persisted, 'I don't just mean a West Indian abroad. Sometimes I miss home so much, just the smell of coffee or floor wax reminds me of it so intensely it is like a physical pain in my belly. No, I mean an outsider. Somebody who sees what happens, somebody who understands but not somebody who is involved . . . not really involved, in life.'

A huge grin spread slowly across Lionel face. 'Aha! Now I've got it. What you mean is, you're not in love!'

'Don't you dare start on that again, Lionel Ramkissoon,' Gloria said, getting up from her seat on his jacket. Lionel pulled her back down.

'The mighty pocket battleship and this slow boat to China?' he chortled. 'Don't worry, man. I like them adoring and willing. You are far too bright and I am far too selfish for us to come to anything. Besides,' he continued confidentially, 'I make a far better friend than lover.'

'Lionel!'

From where they sat, Lionel and Gloria could see the back gate to Kings College. Students returning from the University Library could enter the college that way across one of the many bridges over the Cam. Approaching the bridge now with measured tread was Wisdom, a half-dozen books clutched under his arm.

'Maybe you should ask our fellow student what he thinks you should do,' Lionel suggested mischievously. 'The esteemed Wisdom may know something that we don't.'

'He really does strut along as if he owns the place, doesn't he? Do you know that I've spoken to everyone else in our year except him?'

'Well,' Lionel replied, 'now's your chance. He's going to walk right by us.'

'Don't be silly,' Gloria chided.

'Why not?'

'Do you know, you are absolutely right! Why not? How can life get any worse?' Gloria rose and stepped into the path of the approaching figure. 'Wisdom, I'd like to ask you something.'

'Are you speaking to me?'

'I'm Gloria Carter.'

'I am aware of this.' Wisdom looked distinctly uncomfortable, stopped in his path by this small woman.

'Lionel and I were just wondering why it was that we never seem to talk to one another,' Gloria opened.

Wisdom's eyebrows shot up. 'What is there to talk about?' he enquired, pained at the very thought.

'One across the bows there, battleship. How are you going to respond?' Lionel goaded, grinning.

'Do be quiet!' Gloria snapped. 'We are both law students, we are both from the Commonwealth. Why shouldn't we talk?'

'Ah,' Wisdom said in the tones of someone pointing out the obvious, 'but you are West Indian. I am African.'

'So were several of my ancestors!' Gloria rejoined, glancing to Lionel for support.

'As far as I know, most of my ancestors were from the Punjab, Gloria,' he said apologetically.

'I am,' Wisdom explained patiently, 'of pure blood. You are of mixed blood. In my country, bastards are not permitted to speak with their betters.'

'But we aren't in Nigeria now, Wisdom,' Gloria rallied.

'That is correct,' Wisdom conceded reluctantly. 'Perhaps you would understand why we have not spoken more easily if I say to you that I completely disagree with everything you say about colonial administrations and the law.'

He drew breath and rocked back on his heels, ready to hold forth. 'You generalize,' he accused. 'You say that all colonial societies wish to rule themselves for the same reason. The way the British rule a people who are the descendants of slaves, as in the West Indies, is different from the way they administer a society like the one from which I come.' He smiled pityingly at Gloria before continuing. 'At least Nigeria and Britain share the weight of history – a glorious past in which men have grown out of the very soil of their country.' Gloria heard Lionel trying to repress a snort of laughter. 'We have our own kings and princes. In the West Indies, you were thrown together a few hundred years ago and left to ferment in the sun. What good can come of that?'

'But surely you believe in equality!' Gloria interrupted, shocked.

'If I did, I would not have spent five years at Eton. There are,' he explained, 'men who are destined to lead in life: if one shies away from it, one's place will simply be taken by those less well-equipped for leadership. Perhaps,' he said derisively, 'even by women.'

'You think that I am an upstart?' Gloria asked quietly.

'No point in getting angry,' Lionel warned. 'You asked the man.'

'And I want to hear his answer,' she replied. 'It was a simple enough question. Well, Wisdom?'

'It is not my obligation to explain these things to you,' Wisdom blustered. 'I just hope that now you understand that you do not speak for me when you stand in front of the whole class and say what you are saying. The good thing is, of course,' he said, setting off towards the college gate, 'that no one takes you at all seriously. Good afternoon, Miss Carter.' He did not acknowledge Lionel's presence by look or nod.

'I was wrong,' Gloria whispered, shaken to the core. 'Things could get worse.'

ONE BRIGHT CHILD

* * * * *

Margaret walked backwards ahead of Gloria along the uneven stone floors of the college, stumbling occasionally, but persisting.

'I won't let you go in there, Gloria,' she said as they approached the door of Miss Norman's office. 'Once you tell her, it's irrevocable. Please!' She caught hold of Gloria's hand. 'Think about it for just a little bit longer.'

Summer sunshine streamed in through the high windows along the corridor. In the courtyard beyond, two fire wardens trundled a large metal pump across the grass in preparation for drill that afternoon. A gaggle of nurses sat on the lawn, stockings rolled down and sleeves up, to feel the early summer sun on their skin.

'Stop being silly, Margaret. People are going to stare at us if you don't move out of the way.'

'I don't care,' Margaret said, stumbling on ahead of Gloria.

'Why are you getting so upset? You were always telling me I spent too much time studying,' Gloria objected, trying again to step around her friend.

'But not give up altogether!' Margaret replied. Gloria stopped trying to walk past her and instead looked her friend directly in the eye.

'How many women lawyers do you know?' she asked.

'I'm sure there are lots of them!'

'Answer the question, Margaret,' Gloria insisted.

'You'll be the first. How is that for an answer? You'll be the first lady lawyer that I know. Isn't that worth doing?'

'*You* don't know any,' Gloria stated. '*I* don't know any.'

'So you are just going to give up?' Margaret demanded on the edge of tears.

'I am not giving up! I am,' Gloria said through gritted teeth, 'being sensible. And saving my parents an awful lot of money.' She sidestepped neatly past Margaret and rapped on Miss Norman's office door. 'Realistic, that's the right word!'

Miss Norman opened her office door to see Margaret's very flushed face and Gloria's equally determined one. She looked from one to the other.

'Well?'

'I need to speak to you, Miss Norman,' Gloria said.

'No, she doesn't,' Margaret interrupted, taking hold of Gloria's arm. 'No, you don't, Gloria! I'm sorry we disturbed you, Miss Norman.'

'Just a few minutes, Miss Norman,' Gloria said, detaching herself. 'I'll see you later, Margaret.'

'But . . .' The door swung gently shut in Margaret's face and Gloria disappeared into the depths of Miss Norman's study.

'Do have a seat,' Miss Norman said, pointing her to a worn horsehair sofa. 'Would you like a cup of tea? I find it never fails to soothe the nerves so I keep part of my ration here.' Producing a large Thermos flask and a pair of china tea cups from a small cupboard, Miss Norman made the tea, glancing over occasionally at the young woman who sat looking so determined. Gloria Carter looks tired, she thought. Tired and, like we all do, a lot older than we are.

'I have to admit that I am intrigued to hear what this is all about,' Miss Norman said pleasantly, handing Gloria her cup, 'but before we get to that, I wanted to talk to you about another matter. I'm afraid your father hasn't yet sent your fees for next year. I know the post can sometimes be uncertain, but they should have been here by the end of March and it is now the beginning of May.'

Gloria put the cup down on an end table and folded her hands in her lap to keep them from trembling.

'I don't think they will be coming, Miss Norman.'

'Ah.'

'That's what I wanted to tell you. I won't be finishing my studies. I've decided to go back home. I've thought about it very carefully and—'

A loud knock interrupted her. Margaret's voice could be heard frantically calling Miss Norman. The older woman stood up, frowning.

'What extraordinary behaviour!' she remarked. 'I gather Margaret doesn't agree with your decision?'

'To put it mildly,' Gloria acknowledged.

As Miss Norman opened the door, Margaret tumbled into the room, her face shining; she darted around the room like a squirrel.

'Miss Norman, have you heard? Oh Gloria, isn't it wonderful! It's over! It's finally over!' Tears flowed down her cheeks as she pulled Gloria off the couch and embraced her. 'The wireless was on in the Common Room and we heard Mr Churchill announce it!'

'Over?' Miss Norman breathed.

'The war is over?' Gloria asked. Margaret nodded gleefully. 'At last!'

Margaret danced around the room like a six-year-old. 'No more fire-watches, no more trailer-pump drills, no more blackouts!' she sang. Then she stopped and turned to face Gloria. 'And Jimmy will be coming home!' Both girls realized that Miss Norman had slumped onto the sofa, her head in her hands.

'Miss Norman?' Gloria asked hesitantly. 'Are you OK?'

'It's wonderful! Absolutely and completely bloody marvellous!' she exclaimed, lifting a tear-stained face to theirs.

* * * * *

Later that night, Margaret and Gloria sat together on Midsummer Common watching the sparks from a huge bonfire leap high into the evening sky. They listened to the singing, and watched the huge, swaying crowds of revellers celebrate the end of the war. A huge conga-line snaked around the fire and past them, and everybody in the line looked transformed by their happiness: plain girls looked handsome; weedy lads looked invincible; women exuded sensuality and men explored it greedily. Margaret looked across at Gloria and smiled.

'You realize this is history in the making,' she said.

'I'd get up and join them, but I don't think I can,' Gloria giggled. 'That cider we drank has gone to my head. I feel very wobbly.'

'There's another bonfire on Parker's Piece,' Margaret suggested. 'We could go there.'

'Not with these legs!'

'You know what this means, don't you?' Margaret asked.

'Jimmy is coming home?' Gloria teased.

Margaret blushed. 'My wonderful Jimmy! No, it means, Gloria dear, that you have to persevere against all odds. Bulldog spirit and all that!'

'You never give up, do you?'

'And I never thought you would either. Come on, Gloria. Don't give up. Not yet. Not now. There must be some way to sort things out so you can stay and finish your studies.'

Gloria shook her head.

'You'll hate yourself if you turn tail and run,' Margaret wheedled. The look on Gloria's face told her she had struck a nerve, so she pressed home her advantage.

'The war is over, Gloria – *over*! Thank God. Things can only get better from now on!'

CHAPTER NINE

GIRTON
OCTOBER, 1945

'COME ON, MARGARET. Put your back into it, or we'll be here all day,' Gloria teased as she piled the potatoes she had dug out of the ground neatly beside her. Margaret, face flushed and scarf askew, straightened up and stretched her back.

'I hate potatoes,' she said. 'I shall be very happy if I never dig up, wash off, peel or boil another potato as long as I live,' and she tossed her fork into the dirt. Gloria grinned.

'You won't say that when we tuck into this lot in the middle of a cold January day.'

'Just because some of us spent the summer working on a farm . . .' Margaret sniffed, bending again to her work.

'You missed one there,' Gloria pointed out gleefully.

'. . . Doesn't mean we have to show off. The war's been over for three whole months and the rationing is worse than ever! "And what did you learn at Cambridge, dear?" "Oh, in October, I pulled potatoes, sir, and I learned how to get dressed under the covers on a winter's morning. Oh, and English Literature. I went to a few classes on that in between all the rest!"'

'Don't make fun of my land work,' Gloria said, wrestling a particularly stubborn plant firmly out of the soil. 'I am very proud of my calluses. I wouldn't still be here studying if it weren't for them.'

'*And* Miss Norman. Don't forget her.'

'I would love,' Gloria said, grinning broadly, 'to have seen her face when she lied to the bursar about why my fees hadn't been paid. Father sent them just in time too.'

'Good egg, old Norman,' Margaret agreed. 'Well?'

'Well what?'

'What about me? I knew there had to be a way for you to stay. And I am such a good friend, I won't say "I told you so".'

'Admirable restraint,' Gloria agreed, ducking to avoid the clump of muddy roots Margaret tossed at her. 'Did you collect our tickets when you were in town?'

'I did,' Margaret said. 'Tomorrow night – Beethoven's Sixth. You'll love it. The hall's a bit small, but it should still sound terrific!' Peering up into a lowering sky from which rain had begun to drip, she turned up her collar and surveyed with dismay the half-acre of potatoes yet to be reaped. 'Wonderful. And we're not even halfway through yet!'

A strong smell of mustard pervaded Margaret's room and tickled Gloria's nose as she entered. Swaddled in a blanket, her feet in a basin of steaming water, Margaret sneezed vigorously at the colder air creeping in through the open door.

'I'm sorry,' she said to Gloria who stood, dressed in her smartest navy-blue wool suit, in the doorway. 'I just can't go. I feel as if there is an evil little hobgoblin stamping around behind my eyes. I guess I should have come in out of the rain yesterday.'

'Wrap up warm,' Gloria suggested anxiously. 'We'll take the bus in, instead of cycling.' But Margaret only pulled the blanket more closely around her. 'This was all your idea, going out,' Gloria objected. 'You have to come!'

'Why don't you go alone?' Margaret suggested. Gloria looked very doubtful. 'It's a modern world. Women go to concerts by themselves all the time.' She sneezed another mighty sneeze. 'I'll wait up for you and you can tell me all about it,' she called as Gloria reluctantly closed the door behind her.

Gloria looked up from reading the single sheet of paper on which the programme was printed as the hall darkened and the tuning of instruments on the small platform ceased. The conductor entered to enthusiastic applause and as he raised his baton for silence, Gloria became aware of a young man making his way along the row towards the seat beside her. The conductor froze as the din of bicycle clips clattering to the wooden floor resounded, and turned to glare from under impressive eyebrows at the young man, bottom in the air and rooting along the floor like a flamingo, who searched for them.

'Would you please sit down!' Gloria hissed as he bobbed inches away from her.

'I can't seem to find my other bicycle clip,' he apologized, surfacing.

'The conductor is staring at you!'

'Ah, there it is,' the young man said, smiling shyly at her. 'By your foot. No, the left one. Would you pass it for me please?'

'Yes,' Gloria whispered sharply, 'if you'll just sit down!' Annoyed mutterings behind her told Gloria that she was not the only one who felt this way. Bicycle clips stowed in his pocket, the young man eventually sat still, looking eagerly towards the stage. Several times during the performance, Gloria found herself glancing over at him, becoming aware of his breathing and the scent of soap and tobacco that emanated from him.

After the final notes had died away and the applause had stopped, the audience stood, donning coats and scarves, making their way towards the exit.

'The question is,' the young man said in Gloria's ear, 'whether or not his deafness could actually have enhanced his writing.'

'I beg your pardon?'

'Beethoven's deafness,' he said, following her along the row of seats to the aisle.

'Do you always talk to perfect strangers?' Gloria asked, trying to look disapproving.

'Depends on how perfect they are, I suppose,' he answered, poker-faced.

'Oh, no!' Gloria cried. 'A man who puns!'

'I've tried getting treatment for it. It's probably terminal.' The apologetic voice belied the twinkle in his eye.

'Maybe he heard it all in his head when he was writing,' she volunteered as they emerged through the main door into the street. 'Maybe he didn't need to hear it to create it.'

'Ah,' said the man, producing a small flashlight from his pocket, 'but are things ever really as good as you imagine them to be? Perhaps everything we taste, and smell and touch is really a sensation produced by our imagination. Perhaps imagination is all we have.' People emerging from the concert hall streamed around them in the shadows.

'Can't be,' Gloria disagreed. 'There must be some context for the imagination. We imagine words we would like to say: we have to learn how to speak to even know what words are.' The young man nodded, looking thoughtful.

'You're not Haile Selassie's daughter, are you?' he asked suddenly.

'What?'

'Haile Selassie's daughter. I heard she was studying here.'

'I'm afraid not,' Gloria said. 'No one of such importance.'

'Philosophy?' he asked after a moment of silence. The street was nearly empty.

'Law.'

'Economics, me.'

'With a taste for classical music,' Gloria rejoined. That twinkle returned to his eyes.

'Just a taste,' he said, 'but my Bach is worse than my bite.'

'That was abominable!' Gloria laughed.

'I know – I'm sorry. It happens when I'm nervous. A defence mechanism, I suppose. Like flak.'

'Not quite that bad,' Gloria said comfortingly. 'More like an intellectual St Vitus's Dance.' Each could see the other's smile in the street-light and a moment of silence fell between them.

'My bike is that way,' Gloria said. 'So I'll say good night then.'

'Of course. Yes. Right. Mine's that way,' he replied. 'Good night then.'

As she straddled her bike, ready to mount and ride off, Gloria heard an urgent clicking of bicycle spokes approaching her.

'Wait!' the young man called. 'I won't let you go like that!'

Wheeling his bike along, he ran towards her, the bike weaving unsteadily in the pool of light from his cycle lamp. Five yards before he caught up to her he stumbled and fell over the front wheel, landing in a spectacular heap at her feet.

'Are you all right?' Gloria asked.

'Skinned my shin, I think,' he said, pulling up one trouser leg to examine it. 'Yes, I have skinned it.'

'I have the very strong feeling that you and your bicycle are fundamentally incompatible. Bicycles, bicycle clips . . .'

He grinned up at her, disarmingly. 'Oh, I dropped the clips deliberately so I could talk to you at the concert,' he said.

'Did you?'

'The thing is,' he said, standing up and facing her, 'look, if I had ridden off I would never have had a chance to ask you your name or where I could find you, so I had to turn back.'

'You are,' Gloria said, realizing that she was feeling distinctly breathless, 'the strangest man.'

'Of course I am not implying that you have to tell me who you are. I just thought that I would miss my chance if I didn't at least try to find out. So I came back.' He hesitated briefly then continued. 'And I'm asking.'

'I think I need to know a little bit more about you first,' Gloria said, becoming aware that they were alone in the street. She still felt distinctly breathless.

'George Compton of Burton-on-Trent,' he said with a small bow. 'Won scholarships to both the distinguished Burton Grammar School and Gonville and Caius College but was called up before I could begin my studies here in Cambridge. Served in North Africa and France in the Signals Division. This is my demob suit, my only suit. Son of a brewery clerk and a mother who sent me to elocution lessons the moment she heard I had made it to grammar school.'

'Our mothers sound as if they would have a lot in common,' Gloria said, smiling. They fell into another silence, this time softer than the first.

'Why don't I see you home?' George volunteered.

'All the way to Girton?' Gloria looked surprised by his offer. 'It's miles out of your way.'

'Oh, good,' he said. Pushing their bikes, they followed the beams of their bicycle lamps.

'I'm Gloria Carter,' Gloria said.

'Why was that seat beside you empty?' George asked, glancing at her. 'Were you supposed to have come with someone?'

'The seat you barged your way into?' Gloria teased.

'*Carpe diem*. Besides, you haven't answered my question.'

'That seat was for my friend Margaret.'

'Obviously a woman with a wonderful sense of timing,' George grinned.

'She didn't come because she had a terrible cold!'

'Now,' George said as they approached the bottom of Castle Hill on the way out of the town centre towards Girton. 'I want to hear about your life from start to finish, but it doesn't have to be in any particular sequence because I like association rather than linearity as a narrative form.'

'But linearity gives it structure,' Gloria puffed as the road steepened. 'Drives the narrative in a way that the reader can easily understand.'

'Aha,' rejoined George, 'but should understanding *be* made easy? What does the reader gain if he is not challenged by what he reads?'

'He or she,' Gloria remarked. 'Besides, I'm not saying it should only be easy. I'm saying that there are codes by which we communicate, and if we don't use them, we risk being misunderstood.'

'But surely the job of the writer is to widen those codes, to challenge them?'

'But you can't challenge them,' Gloria said as they topped the brow of the hill, 'until you know exactly what purpose they serve. You have to start from what exists conventionally before you start disobeying the conventions.'

The road to Girton lay open before them. No longer in the shadow of college buildings and shops, it was lit by a milky half-moon. George stopped and turned to face Gloria and waited until she too stopped and looked up at him.

'Perhaps,' he said thoughtfully, 'there is a truth beyond convention that we arrive at through instinctive decision making.'

Gloria felt as though it took a physical effort to look away from that gentle gaze. She began pushing her bike towards Girton again and heard when he followed her.

'Why did you want to sit down next to me?' she asked. 'Why are you talking to me now?'

'Why,' he replied, 'are you talking to me?' The bicycle spokes clicked loudly in the silence that followed his question.

'It seems right, somehow,' Gloria replied eventually. Suddenly she laughed. 'I feel as if I'm sitting barefoot in my mango tree at home again. As if I can breathe.'

George smiled too. 'There's a production of *Uncle Vanya* by the Drama Society at the end of the month,' he said. 'I think we should go to that.'

Margaret dreamt that someone was rapping on her skull with icy fingers until she woke up and realized that it was Gloria knocking on the window over her head.

'Come *on*, Margaret. Let me in. It's freezing out here!' she whispered as loudly as she dared.

'If Miss Norman catches *you* coming in ...' Margaret replied as she slid the sash window open, '... and catches *me* letting you in at this hour, we will both be rusticated!'

Scrambling through the open window with undignified haste, Gloria landed in a heap in Margaret's bed. As quickly and quietly as she could, Margaret closed the window behind her and turned to face her friend who was heading, shoes in hand, towards the door.

'You think you can climb in through my window grinning like the cat who got the cream and not tell me about it?' she demanded, her voice husky from coughing. 'It's past three o'clock!'

'There's nothing to tell,' Gloria replied.

'Will you stop grinning like that!' Margaret demanded, grabbing Gloria by the sleeve as she tried to slip through the door.

'I've just met the strangest man.'

'Don't tell me that is where you were all evening! What about the concert?'

'He walked me home after the concert and then we walked back into town because we didn't want to stop talking and then we walked back out again.'

Margaret, listening carefully, climbed back into bed and pulled her blankets up to her chin. 'Sounds completely insane.'

'It didn't feel insane,' Gloria smiled. 'It felt . . . it felt right.'

Margaret's eyes narrowed. 'You've never behaved like this before,' she said suspiciously. 'For heaven's sake, Gloria, you're a graduate. You're supposed to be the sensible one, the mature one. You're supposed to give me good advice, not behave like this!'

'Be your – what was that expression you used – *barrage balloon* to keep all the flirtatious pilots away?'

'Exactly!'

'War's over, Margaret, and this is one barrage balloon that wants to do a little flying of her own. I think I deserve it. Besides,' she said, 'I don't think he's interested in me that way, so you don't need to worry.'

Margaret felt her ears turning red. 'I didn't mean . . . I'm happy you've met someone, but – well, it's out of character, that's all.'

Gloria came and sat on the bed beside Margaret, smiling ruefully at her.

'When I'm around him, I don't have to pretend I am less intelligent than I really am, I don't have to pretend that where I come from and who I am is less important because I am not English.'

'And is that what you do with me?'

'Sometimes.'

Margaret looked down and began picking at the rough stitching along the edge of her blanket.

'I never realized that was how you felt,' she said. 'I hate whoever he is already.'

'No, you don't.' Gloria patted Margaret's hand comfortingly, smiling at her when she looked up. 'It was a lovely evening but I probably won't ever see him again. This is my final year, remember. There's work to be done.' Standing up, she yawned and stretched. 'Thanks for letting me back in. Now go to sleep. And stop gawping at me like that. It makes you look most unattractive!' she said cheekily, and slipped quickly out of the door so that the pillow Margaret threw at her thudded against it harmlessly.

It took George several anxious minutes before he spotted Gloria amongst the crowd of undergraduates making their way from the Law Faculty towards their colleges at lunch-time.

'I thought you would never turn up,' he gasped, catching up with her breathlessly. 'I've been hanging around outside the Law Faculty for so long, I thought the proctors were going to ask me to move on!'

Amazed at the behaviour of her heartbeat at the sound of his voice, Gloria struggled for the kind of dignity Mary Datchelor and Albertha Carter had schooled into her.

'And why on earth did you do that?' she asked. George looked puzzled, a little offended.

'You know perfectly well why.' Looking down he noticed for the first time how scuffed his sturdy brown shoes were, and continued in a mumble. 'We never finished discussing whether Orwell was right about the Spanish Civil War.'

'No, I suppose we didn't.' There was almost no disappointment in Gloria's polite voice.

'I'm sorry – I don't flirt very well. Don't look so offended,' George pleaded, beginning to smile.

'I'm not offended.'

'Good,' George said, taking her arm and following the flow of hungry students. 'Does that mean you will come to the cinema with me this evening?'

'What's playing?' Gloria asked, aware of several pairs of eyes watching them.

'I haven't the slightest idea but I thought it sounded better than saying I wanted to talk to you all evening. Will you come?'

The temptation to say yes immediately was unbearable.

'I have an awful lot of work to do.'

'Of course,' George agreed, letting go of her arm. 'Graduate student and all that. Of course.'

He looked hurt and terribly vulnerable. Gloria realized that the standard rules of engagement did not apply to this situation. It felt dangerous, as if someone had told her she could fly and now was asking her to leap off a cliff.

'I was going over to the University Library. You could walk with me, if you like.'

The smile that spread over George's face reminded Gloria of the way a sunflower presents its heart to the beating sun. George gave an audible sigh of relief and became once again the young man who had walked Gloria home two nights before.

'It seems to me that the problem with war,' he said, as they headed along the cobbled streets of Kings Parade, 'is that it is never as glorious or as noble in reality as it is in concept. The details of everyday survival overwhelm the bigger issues, don't they?'

Radnor   *November 17th, 1945*
Half Way Tree Post Office
St Andrew

Dear Gloria,

It is all well and good to write and say you have met a young man and how nice it is to sit and talk with him about this and that.

Remember, at your age, a friendship between a man and a woman can often be seen as something more. It does the man no harm but it does the lady a great deal!

I have always trusted that you were too commonsensical to get yourself involved with a man who is going to lead you into the ways of sin and you claim he does not think of you in that way. Since you have devoted yourself to your studying for so long, I am not sure you are the best judge of such matters. Thoughts of the flesh are never far from any man's mind in my experience, and I know the war has heated up the blood of a lot of young women. Please, please think what would happen to you if you were to slip up and ruin your life with the wrong sort of man. Your letter sounded quite giddy!

I have written to Mrs Thompson by the same post and asked her if she would call on you at Girton. I think that this would be a good time to introduce her to this young man. After all, she has lived in England for years. She will know what this young man really wants.

News from home now: Mrs Marley is in a dreadful state. Her daughter's baby was born and although he is a handsome little chap, there is little doubt in my mind that her son-in-law is not her grandson's father. What a hell and powderhouse! Father says I must mind my own business, but how can I? The rumours are spreading faster than love bush on a hibiscus hedge!

Father brought a couple of pounds of coffee back from his last surveying job in the Blue Mountains. I've roasted it and will send some to you as I hear coffee is in short supply. There are still shortages here, of course, but things are slowly going back to normal. Even the prisoners of war have gone. Most of them, at least. Some had settled in quite happily and said they'd like to stay!

Father says he will wire some money to you by the end of the month, but he thought it more important to pay the fees first. His own father wore himself out cutting cane for little and nothing all his life (he died just before you were born so you didn't know him). I think it upset Father to hear you worked as a farm labourer in the summer. He looks tired sometimes but at least the Austin is back on the road and those smelly mules have gone from the back garden!

Mother

P.S. Mr Ashenheim often asks how you are getting on. He says he has had several enquiries after positions in his chambers but wishes to wait until he has spoken to you before he decides. I am almost used to the idea of having a barrister for a daughter now (especially after what happened to poor Mrs Marley!).

'Gloria! Slow down there, battleship!' Lionel called, trotting after Gloria as she moved briskly through her fellow undergraduates.

'I wish you wouldn't call me that in public,' Gloria hissed at him as he caught up to her.

'You were sailing through that crowd with such determination, nothing else was appropriate,' he replied. Today he was resplendent in a vivid blue waistcoat and matching silk cravat under a long black cloak, and stood out like a peacock among sparrows.

'I'm late, that's all,' Gloria explained.

'I'll walk with you.'

'How do you know what direction I'm going in?' she enquired.

Lionel grinned with satisfaction. 'Because it is the same direction you have taken every day after lectures for the last month. I thought I'd come with you to meet the mystery man at Gonville and Caius today.'

'Have you been following me?' Gloria asked angrily.

'Is that hostility? Defensiveness, perhaps?'

'We're just friends, Lionel. It's not what you're thinking.'

Lionel raised an astonished eyebrow. 'How can I think anything when I haven't even met the man?'

'There he is.'

George was standing outside the porter's lodge of Gonville and Caius, wrapped in his college scarf, his nose buried deep in a book. Lionel took a long look.

'Interesting jacket,' he volunteered.

'I never said he was as sartorially accomplished as you are,' Gloria snapped.

'Definitely defensive,' Lionel concluded. Looking up, George saw them approaching and thrust his book into his jacket pocket. Lionel observed the look that passed between Gloria and George with interest and shook George's proffered hand warmly.

'You must be Lionel. I'm George Compton.'

'Lionel suffers from an overwhelming curiosity, I'm afraid. He invited himself along,' Gloria said apologetically.

'And do I pass muster?' George asked Lionel.

'I didn't come to pass judgment, man.'

'Of course you did. You wanted to know if I was just some English lad on a demob scholarship with a taste for dusky maidens.' George was standing squarely in front of Lionel, toe to toe, eye to eye.

'George!' Gloria remonstrated.

'Am I wrong, Lionel?'

'It has been known to happen. We West Indians are rather proud of our little pocket battleship here. Even in the bastion of the Law Faculty, she is becoming rather a star, you see. So we just wanted to make sure she was being treated with the respect she deserves.'

'And when exactly did you plan on showing that respect? George asked, straight-faced. 'Before or after you asked her to do your mending for you?'

'Will you both stop talking about me as if I was not here? You look like a pair of scrawny barnyard roosters scrapping over a worm!' Gloria interjected.

Lionel looked surprised. 'Scrawny? An unkind cut, Gloria.'

'Besides,' George agreed, 'there's nothing like a good scrap to keep the blood pumping. And I suspect his motives were honourable.'

Lionel looked from one to the other and a huge smile crept across his face. 'George,' he said, shaking his hand, 'the woman should have brought you around and introduced you ages ago. I don't understand why she is hiding you in the shadows.' He gathered the folds of his cloak around him. 'Must dash,' he continued. 'Managed to purloin rather a nice bottle of brandy so I thought I'd invite a few friends round to my digs to share it. Sunday afternoon at my place? Four-ish?' he called, striding off towards the Senate House.

'He followed me,' Gloria apologized as they set off in the opposite direction.

'*Have* you been hiding me in the shadows?' George asked quietly.

'Don't pay any attention to Lionel. He has a great flare for dramatic overstatement. He will make a great barrister.'

'You haven't answered my question,' George persisted, stepping neatly out of the path of a cyclist pelting along the Senate House Passage, gown flapping in the breeze.

'It was a silly question,' Gloria parried.

'There are,' George began thoughtfully, 'three possible interpretations. One: that you were so happy when we were alone together, the thought of introducing me to your friends never crossed your mind.' He glanced across at Gloria, but she was examining the cuff of her coat with some care. 'Two: you want to be with me but you aren't sure of me and you don't want to make a fool of yourself by introducing me into your life before you are sure of what my intentions are.' Gloria felt his eyes on her face, but could not raise her eyes to meet his. 'Or three: you have no notion of introducing me to anyone, ever, because I am just not that important to you.'

'George, I—'

'I don't think number three is true. I know you care for me,' George said and was rewarded with an audible sigh of relief from Gloria. 'And I don't flatter myself that I am so devastatingly charming that number one is true.' Glancing over at her, George saw the beginnings of a smile. 'Which leaves number two. You don't feel sure of me.' The silence that followed these words was as heavy and fragile as a glass millefiori paperweight.

'I don't know if I want to talk about this,' Gloria whispered. She pulled up the collar of her coat, thinking how much colder and more penetrating the winter wind now felt.

'We talk about everything else under the sun,' George replied. 'Why not this?'

'I'm not sure I want to hear what you are going to say. Can't we just go on as we are? Why is it so urgent?'

George stopped and took her hands, oblivious of the curious looks he was getting. Through their gloves, Gloria thought she could feel how strong his hands were, how urgently he held onto her.

'I have to go away for a few days. I'm going home. There are some things I need to do there – someone I need to see. I'll be back by the weekend. My tutor has given me permission so I won't be AWOL.'

Gloria nodded. 'Mrs Thompson is coming to Cambridge this weekend. She wants to meet you. In fact, she probably doesn't want to meet you but my mother has ordered her to come and look you over.'

'I'll scrub up and look presentable then,' he said, squeezing her hands reassuringly before letting them go.

'It's amazing how my mother still manages to run my life

from thousands of miles away,' Gloria observed as they began walking again.

'Don't worry,' George said kindly, 'I'll be there to hold your hand. I just need to get this trip home out of the way. I'll probably arrive back having drunk far too much beer and full of all the food my mother can scrape together with her ration book!'

CHAPTER TEN

GEORGE CHARGED THROUGH the door of Gloria's college room and skidded to a halt.

'Ah, good. She's not here yet,' he observed, straightening his tie. 'I thought I might be late. All set?' Gloria looked up from the plate of half a dozen plain biscuits she was rearranging and smiled nervously.

'I made coffee,' she said. 'And Margaret gave me a few of her biscuits. How do I look?'

'She really makes you uncomfortable, doesn't she?'

'It's silly, isn't it?' Gloria sighed and then began re-arranging the biscuits again.

'Do I pass muster?' George asked, standing to attention.

'Of course you do,' Gloria smiled reluctantly. 'Besides, you don't need to worry. I said in my letter that we were just friends, so you are quite safe from the worst of the interrogation.' George raised a sceptical eyebrow, but said nothing.

Mrs Thompson burst into the room in a sweep of fox tails and hat feathers. She took Gloria's hand and patted her cheek, then began a scrutiny of George that soon had the colour creeping up from the collar he was suddenly aware of as threadbare, towards his cheeks.

'What a lovely young woman you've grown into,' Mrs Thompson opined as Gloria set about pouring the coffee. 'That smell reminds me of sitting with your mother on the front verandah of the house at Half Way Tree.'

'Every time I make it, an awful lot of people seem to find some reason to pop into my room, so now I just save it for special occasions. Mother sent it for me,' Gloria said, handing Mrs Thompson the cup and sitting opposite her. George, hands thrust deep in his pockets, stood behind Gloria's chair. 'I hope you had a pleasant journey?'

'Oh, very pleasant, mi love. Some of the road signs have been put back up so we found our way quite easily. You are a good way out of town here though. And don't get me wrong, but there is somet'ing a little dismal about the buildings.'

'I was told they were designed by the same man who designed Dartmoor Prison. Perhaps he thought it would protect Girtonian virtue.' Mrs Thompson nodded politely, sipped her coffee and set it down. She turned to George.

'Tell me about yourself,' she commanded, but then continued speaking as George drew breath to do so. 'I am a very close friend of Gloria's mother – I'm sure Gloria has told you she spent many school holidays with me before the war – and I am acting *in loco parentis*. Mrs Carter will expect chapter and verse when I report back to her.'

'What particularly did you want to know?' George asked.

'Don't play coy with me, young man.'

'I'm not. I'm just not sure what you want to know.' Gloria picked up the plate of biscuits and thrust them at Mrs Thompson, who ignored them.

'Your prospects. Your aspirations. Your family background,' Mrs Thompson recited. 'Gloria is from a very well-known family and her father is a wealthy man.'

'Mrs Thompson, please ...' Gloria was deeply embarrassed.

'You just leave this to me, child,' Mrs Thompson replied, eyes still on George.

'You don't understand ...' Gloria tried again.

'Oh, I want to hear what she has to say, Gloria,' George intervened, bristling.

'I have lived in England for many years, George, and I am well aware that there are many kinds of Englishman . . .' She paused for effect. '. . . and not all of them are honourable!'

George laughed. 'You want to know if my intentions are honourable?' he asked.

'Would the pair of you please stop discussing me as if I were not here?' Gloria demanded. 'I'm sorry, Mrs Thompson, I thought you came here to meet George, to see how I was. If what you really came to do was to disapprove of everything without even listening to what we have to say . . .'

'Are you,' her visitor asked in tones both dignified and offended, 'asking me to leave?' Gloria felt herself folding under the weight of implication.

'No, of course not.'

'Because,' Mrs Thompson continued, 'my mother always said that if you have to whisper things behind people's backs then you were up to no good.' Gloria looked desperately to George.

'Oh, for God's sake,' he burst out, 'this is just ridiculous! You want to know what my intentions are? I'll tell you. I couldn't have asked Gloria to marry me before even if I wanted to, because I was engaged to someone else.'

Gloria heard Mrs Thompson's triumphant rejoinder as if from a great distance.

'Now we are finding out who this young man really is, Gloria! I told you to leave it to me!'

'I didn't tell her I was engaged, because I knew she wouldn't see me if I did.'

'George,' Gloria said, forcing the word through her tightened throat.

'Don't look so stricken, Gloria!' Mrs Thompson admonished. 'At least you found out before it is too—' She paused, and sprang from her chair to come and stand in front of Gloria's seat. 'Dear heaven, it isn't too late, is it?'

'Too late for what?' Gloria asked. Mrs Thompson's voice dropped to an intense whisper as she turned a broad back to George.

'You haven't engaged in . . . unladylike behaviour, have you?'

'In *what*? No. No, of course not!'

Mrs Thompson turned to face George, arms akimbo. 'I think it is time you left, young man,' she said.

'That's why I went back to Burton-on-Trent, Gloria.' George found himself being pushed towards the door by the visitor's inexorable presence.

'I don't care to repeat myself, young man. If you do not leave here this minute, I shall call the porter to put you out! Stand behind me, my dear,' she ordered as George tried in vain to push past her to Gloria's side. 'Don't let him approach you. Remember, Gloria, this is a man who has lied to you!'

'Oh, for God's sake, will you just shut up!' George shouted, goaded to the limit of his patience. A loaded silence fell. 'I've had enough of hysterical bloody females for a life-time this week!' He pushed unceremoniously past Mrs Thompson who stood rigid with shocked disapproval and took Gloria's hand. 'I went to Burton to tell her I couldn't marry her, that the engagement was off, because I wanted to marry *you*, Gloria – if you would have me.'

Mrs Thompson's mouth closed with a snap and with a small creak of her corsets, she snatched their hands apart.

'A likely story! You don't fool me for one minute, George Compton!'

'Marry you?' Gloria mumbled.

'You can see why I had to tell her first, before I could say anything to you?' George asked. 'You would think I was holding her over your head. Say "yes" or I'll go off and marry someone else. I want you to say "yes" without duress.'

'I'll have you know that she has not the smallest intention of marrying you,' Mrs Thompson rallied.

'Yes,' Gloria said.

'Yes?' George gulped.

'Yes!?' Mrs Thompson thundered.

'Yes.'

'Now, Gloria, you have no idea where this young man has actually been or what his real intentions are. He lied to you, remember? Gloria!' she shouted as the young woman walked straight past her into George's embrace.

'I thought so. I hoped so – but I wasn't sure,' George said, folding her in.

Mrs Thompson scratched around them like an irate peahen. 'But you've only known him a couple of weeks! Your mother will want to know much more about him before she decides whether he is suitable or not. He's probably just after your father's money to buy himself a start in life! He doesn't,' she said as a last desperate effort, 'even own a decent suit!'

'She's right about that, at least,' George chuckled.

'With the greatest respect in the world, Mrs Thompson, there is nothing you, my mother, or anyone else can say that will change my mind.'

Mrs Thompson took her gloves from her handbag and slowly drew them on, the picture of offended dignity.

'So you are going to marry this man.'

'As soon as possible?' George asked.

'As soon as possible,' Gloria agreed, happily.

Mrs Thompson adjusted her hat and slid its long, gleaming hatpin back into place to anchor it.

'You make your father lay out thousands of pounds to send you to university, spend years upon years studying, just to marry the first common little Englishman that asks you?'

'Yes, Mrs Thompson.'

'We'll see', the woman said grimly, turning in the doorway, 'what your mother has to say about this!' And she slammed the door petulantly behind her.

'I'm sorry,' George said, pulling Gloria close. 'It wasn't very romantic.'

'No,' she agreed, 'but it was wonderful.' When she came up for air and before he could kiss her again, she made sure to ask him how soon was as soon as possible?

A twelve-piece dance orchestra played discreetly and conversations were soft and punctuated by laughter. Brass gleamed and wood glowed as waiters moved between the tables at the Café Royale. An oasis of pre-war elegance a world away from the grimy London streets outside, the Café was nearly full. People were paying good money to escape for an afternoon from the realities of rationing and shortages.

Lionel, George and Gloria watched Margaret's face in amusement as the dessert trolley trundled to a halt beside their table. She chose a large cream cake and dug into it almost as soon as the waiter slid it onto her plate.

'This is just so good,' she moaned. 'I have never tasted food this good before.' She wiped a smidgeon of cream from her chin. 'I know it's wrong, but I've decided to elope with the pastry cart!'

At Lionel's signal, a waiter approached with a bottle of wine and four glasses. There were a few glances from the surrounding tables, some envious, many disapproving, of their evident bonhomie.

'I think we should drink a toast, don't you?' Lionel enquired of them all.

'Absolutely,' Margaret agreed. 'To Gloria and George!'

'The most magnificently foolhardy couple in the world. Long life, good health, wealth and happiness. It was an honour to be your best man, George!' Lionel said.

'And thank you so much for asking me to be your bridesmaid, Gloria. I would never have got to wear this divine frock of yours if I hadn't,' Margaret added.

George tapped his tea cup with his spoon. 'My wife and I . . .'

'Well said, man. Well said!' Lionel encouraged.

George smiled at Gloria, reaching for her hand. 'My wife and I would like to thank both of you for giving up your Saturday afternoon to trundle all the way up to London with us to witness our wedding.'

'Wild horses,' Lionel replied, 'would not have kept us away.'

'And thank you so much for this wonderful tea, Lionel,' Gloria said. 'We could never have afforded anything like this ourselves.'

Lionel, beaming, shook his head as if to say it was nothing. 'Oh, just watching Margaret's face whenever the cream cakes pass is reward enough,' he demurred, tweaking his crimson bow tie into place. 'I think this is one of the best ways I've found so far to spend my father's money!'

'I'd love to be there when you break the news to Miss Norman. She'll turn absolutely puce!' Margaret chortled, scraping the last of the jam and cream from her plate.

George glanced quickly at Gloria. 'Actually, Margaret, we aren't going to tell Miss Norman.'

'Why on earth not?' their friend demanded, puzzled.

'Because she'd have to inform George's college, you see,' Gloria explained. 'And a married man can't live in college rooms. We'd have to move out and find somewhere to live. We don't have the money or the time for that right now.'

'We thought we'd wait until the exams were over,' George added.

'You know what is going to happen, don't you?' Margaret

112

asked Lionel. 'I'm the one who is going to get in trouble over all this.'

'You?'

'Me,' she confirmed. 'Because I'm the one with the room on the ground floor this year, so you know through whose window certain illicit visitors will be wanting to climb.'

Lionel's bark of laughter made several heads turn to see what had so amused the motley occupants of their table.

'George? Is this true?'

'Don't answer that, my love,' Gloria intervened smartly. 'It is a leading question and one that may be incriminating.'

'I think I should follow my barrister's advice, don't you?'

'You sly dog!' Lionel crowed. 'But what if your college finds out, young man? Don't you have to sign in at nights? How are you going to explain *that*?'

George smiled and raised his glass. 'We'll just have to risk it for these last few weeks of term. Come on, drink up. We're celebrating, remember?'

Sitting in the old armchair by the window of Gloria's college room, George enjoyed the early summer sunshine that streamed in almost as much as he enjoyed watching his wife pace up and down to the door and back, her forehead wrinkled by a small frown.

'It's not "just a viva", George. You know what it means when the examiners ask you to come in for a viva. It means you've failed your exams but they are trying to give you a last chance!'

'Is that what they said to you?'

'No, of course not, but ...' She stopped pacing and flopped despairingly down in the chair opposite him.

'Why don't you ask then? Even if you've done badly ...'

'I have – I know I have. I've let everybody down.'

'. . . wouldn't it be better to know than to be in this kind of torment?'

Gloria shook her head vigorously. 'This may be torment, but at least there is still a chance . . .'

George leaned forward and took her hands in his. 'No matter how you're feeling right now,' he said soothingly, 'that isn't going to change your marks. The worst that can happen is that you've failed. You can try again.'

'No,' Gloria said. 'I can't.'

'Of course you can. Half the lawyers practising today had to do some part of their course over,' he tried to reassure her, but she pulled her hands out of his grasp and went to her desk.

'It's not that, love,' she said unfolding a letter that lay on top of a stack of books. 'This came this morning.'

Radnor   *May 13th, 1946*
Half Way Tree Post Office
St Andrew

Dear Gloria,

Since you have seen fit to get married in some registry office without even the courtesy of a by your leave, I think it is only right and proper that you should take responsibility for what you did. I have discussed this with Father and he agrees with me that if you choose to be a married woman, you are no longer our responsibility. It is up to your husband to support you from now on.

I don't know what I have done for you to treat me like this. A daughter's wedding is one of the most important days in a mother's life and I have been denied this by my only child. Mrs Marley says that it looks very bad to be married so hastily and already there are rumours beginning to fly about the place, just when Father has been invited to Kings House to be congratulated on his contribution to his profession by the Governor himself. I hope he does not run into

Mr Ashenheim there, because I don't know how he will tell him what you have done.

If you make your bed, you must lie in it, my dear. Mrs Thompson writes me that this young man has absolutely no manners. I hope you know what you are doing.

Mother

'See?' Gloria asked as George refolded the letter.

'She's right,' he said. 'You are a married woman now, and I am responsible for you. It's time we sorted out our lives together. I've made a decision.'

'No,' Gloria cried, snatching the letter away from him. 'No, you are not even going to think about leaving university and finding a job!'

George smiled ruefully. 'I did think about that for a while, but in the end it didn't make much sense.' Gloria gave a sigh of relief. 'So I've decided to finish my degree in one year instead of two.'

'But . . .'

'I've wasted too much time already, love. I'm twenty-four years old. I don't think I could stand two more years here.'

'And this has nothing to do with supporting me?' Gloria interrogated.

'Nothing at all,' George insisted. 'I have my scholarship money and my tutor says I've won an Exhibition so that should put another fifteen pounds in our pocket.'

'So I'm the one letting the side down.' Gloria turned away and went to look out the window. The chestnut trees stood benevolent guard over the neat rows of burgeoning vegetables. A couple of undergraduates were doing more chatting than weeding in the cabbage patch. Their laughter seemed enviably carefree to Gloria as she stood at her window in the slanting shaft of sunlight. George came to stand behind her, putting his arms around her waist. She leant back against him, tense and still.

'It's a beautiful summer's day. Exams are over. Why don't we go into town? There's something I'd like to show you.'

'But my viva is tomorrow morning.'

'If you don't know it now, you're not going to learn it overnight. Come on, love,' he coaxed, leading her towards the door.

'This better be good, George Compton!'

'This is absolutely awful!'

Standing in the middle of the living room of the flat in Botolph Lane, Gloria looked around her in consternation. The carpet was so threadbare in some places that the floorboards could be seen underneath. A distinct odour of raw meat and offal rose from the butcher's shop downstairs. A set of lopsided shelves were the only furniture in a room whose walls were daubed with uneven coats of what had originally been green paint. It now looked grey.

'The building has no roof,' Gloria pointed out. 'And you can smell the butcher's shop downstairs through the floorboards.'

'The flat upstairs has no roof,' George corrected her. 'At least we have a floor and ceiling between us and the weather. And the butcher says we can have it for little and nothing if we do a few repairs.'

Gloria pushed open the door to the tiny kitchen. Dust had settled on the greasy surface of the cooker, coagulating into a skin so dark as to disguise the appliance's original colour. An inch of mottled water rested comfortably in the sink. It had been there a long time.

'The only other flat we can afford is in Cherry Hinton,' George sighed, 'miles away, I'm afraid. But we can go and look at it, if you'd like.'

'And leave a flat two doors away from Fitzbillies, the best

bakery in Cambridge? Near to three decent bookshops, the market and the Corn Exchange – with King's Parade and Great St Mary's practically on our doorstep?' Gloria asked. 'Never!' She was rewarded by the beatific smile that spread across her husband's face. 'What more,' she asked him, 'could a woman want?'

'I'll tell him we'll take it then,' George beamed. Just then Gloria screamed and ran out of the flat, slamming the door behind her.

'What? What is it?' he asked, alarmed.

'A rat!' Gloria shouted from behind the door. 'Going into the cupboard in the kitchen!'

'Where?' George asked, hunting for it vigorously. 'I don't see anything!'

Gloria opened the flat door and re-entered cautiously. 'It was a huge rat,' she insisted. 'And it looked pregnant.'

'Do you think there'll be an extra charge for pets?' he ventured, looking worried.

'Fool!'

'Fear not, dear lady. With my trusty sword I shall defeat the grisly beast,' he pronounced, galumphing around the flat as if on a hobby horse, 'separating its noggin from its neck with a mighty snicker-snack of my vorpal blade!'

'Don't you dare kill anything in here, George Compton,' Gloria chuckled, still glancing nervously at the cupboard in the corner.

'May I then suggest my mother's remedy?' George enquired, struggling to open the window to cool his ruddied face. 'Stamp firmly twice before you open the cupboard or upon seeing the enemy approaching.'

'And if that doesn't work?' Gloria asked, coming to stand with him at the open window to watch a group of undergraduates in the grip of post-exam euphoria tumble noisily down the lane below.

'Stand on a chair and scream blue murder, of course!'

'We might as well sit in here,' Margaret said, heading for the waiting room at Cambridge station. It was the day after graduation. 'I knew I would be too early for my train.' Putting her hat-box neatly on top of her small suitcase, she sat on the long bench, ankles crossed demurely. Her trunks had been sent home and would be there when she finally arrived. She looked, Gloria observed as she sat beside her, taut as piano wire.

'Jimmy's meeting me in London,' Margaret said nervously. 'We're going to spend the day there before I go home. The Convalescent Home says he should be able to manage it now.' She looked down and checked her nails. 'Jimmy and I were thinking of getting married this summer.'

'You don't sound very sure,' Gloria prompted gently.

'Well, it isn't going to be the nice house and three children for us, is it?' Margaret continued. 'I've applied to do the teaching certificate, so I can go to work if Jimmy can't. He isn't healing as well after the amputation as they'd hoped. They can't say when he'll be truly fit and well.' Margaret smiled at Gloria, dabbing at the corner of one eye.

'You'll make a wonderful teacher,' Gloria assured her.

'You are one of the most charitable people I know. I shall probably make an abominable teacher, but I am determined to try.' Margaret patted Gloria's hand awkwardly. 'I can't believe it is all over. Three years of my life. I shall miss you, Gloria Compton.'

'No, you won't. You'll write regularly. And come and visit. Bring Jimmy.'

'And don't let Lionel lead George astray.'

They heard the rumble of an approaching train.

'I don't think he stands the slightest chance of doing that,' Gloria promised her. They both paused.

'That's my train. I suppose I'd better be on it,' Margaret sighed, breaking the silence.

'Right. You can't keep Jimmy waiting, after all!'

Margaret didn't look back at Gloria until her cases were stowed overhead and she was seated on the train.

'Write to me!' Gloria mouthed as the train pulled out. Tears snaked down Margaret's cheeks as she smiled and waved her farewell. 'Write me.'

Gloria carefully folded her college scarf and put it among the woollens she was packing away in one of her trunks. Despite her best efforts to be orderly, her attempts at packing had resulted in a room that resembled the aftermath of a hurricane – piles of clothes, books and papers scattered everywhere. Miss Norman stepped over the nearest pile as she entered and looked around her in amusement.

'It always amazes me how books and papers accumulate. They must be like mushrooms growing in dark corners. I'll never fit it all in,' Gloria said despairingly.

'Well, you're not going far so it won't be too much of a problem, will it? Above the butcher's shop in Botolph Lane, I believe?' Gloria looked up sharply at Miss Norman's tone.

'I know I should have told you I'd married George, Miss Norman, but it was so close to exams and we would have had to move out and find digs and we had nowhere to go . . .'

'Wouldn't that have been a good reason to wait until term was over before getting married?' Miss Norman chided. 'You could have been sent down, both of you, with no hope of getting your degrees!'

'I don't think even that would have stopped us,' Gloria said quietly.

'Do you know, I think this is one of the most romantic things that has happened since I have been at Girton?'

'I surprised myself, Miss Norman,' Gloria admitted with a rueful smile.

'If I don't see you before you go down, I want to wish you all the very best, Gloria,' Miss Norman said, extending a brisk hand. 'I think your result was exactly what you deserved: very fair indeed.'

Gloria found herself gasping for breath. 'They have posted the results?' she whispered.

'They were up when I passed the Senate House this morning.'

'How did I do? No – don't tell me. I can't bear it. Yes, tell me ... no!' Miss Norman looked intensely amused by Gloria's indecision. 'If it's a lower second or a third, I won't accept it!' the young woman declared. 'I'll find a way to do it again.'

'I tell you what, my dear,' Miss Norman suggested, 'why don't you ride into town and take a look for yourself? The exercise will calm you down.'

'Yes,' Gloria said, skittling down her piled possessions in her haste to reach the door. 'I'll get George to come with me.'

'There's a letter for you at the Porter's Lodge,' Miss Norman called after her. 'You can collect that on your way. It looks as though it's from Jamaica.'

'Wonderful,' Gloria muttered to herself, grabbing her bike out of the rack in the courtyard. 'Just what I need. Another letter from my mother telling me what a disappointment I am to her.'

This is not a good sign, she thought to herself as she pedalled along the main road that led from Girton to the heart of Cambridge.

Definitely not a good sign!

CHAPTER ELEVEN

GEORGE TUGGED GENTLY to see whether there was any chance of Gloria releasing her grip on his fingers. There wasn't.

'You can't stand outside the Senate House with your eyes shut for ever, love. The University proctors will come and move us on.'

'Can you see my name?' Gloria asked, eyes screwed tight.

'Yes, right beside all the others who took their LLB.' Two undergrads clad in striped college blazers glanced curiously across at the pair of them. George smiled and shrugged and they moved off. 'You're going to have to open your eyes sometime. And I might need to restart the circulation in my hand at some point too.'

'I'm sorry!' Gloria said, letting him go. 'Did I hurt you?'

'Oh, the bruises around my ring finger should heal in a month or two.'

Gloria squared her shoulders and opened her eyes. 'They would have to post the results outside the Senate House right in the middle of town so that everybody can see what a fool I have made of myself,' she muttered, scanning the results.

'Some of us would be delighted with first-class honours,' George remarked. 'I know I was.'

'A first! You mean I . . . A first!' Gloria traced her name on the lists suspended in front of her. 'Do you know what this means? You're married to a lawyer. Well, almost a lawyer – I still have to be called to the Bar, but . . .' Happiness shone through her face like a candle through a Chinese lantern. 'Oh, George!'

She pulled her husband close and just as they were about to kiss, an icy voice spoke.

'I can't say that I entirely approve of such public displays of affection, Mr Compton,' it said.

'Dr Weekes! Gloria, this is my tutor, Dr Weekes. I'm sorry, Gloria just got her results.'

'And they were?' asked Dr Weekes, polishing his pince-nez before balancing them on the bridge of his nose and subjecting Gloria to a penetrating stare.

'First-class honours, Dr Weekes,' George said proudly.

'How delightful for her.' He slid his pince-nez into a pocket of the waistcoat he always wore no matter how warm the weather. 'I shall expect both of you for a celebratory sherry at five – in the same rooms where we meet for tutorials, Mr Compton,' he informed them.

'I don't know if we can . . .'

'It was,' Dr Weekes cut in, 'a statement, Mr Compton. Not a suggestion. Not even an invitation. Please remember, I deplore tardiness. Good day.'

The young couple watched Dr Weekes walk away from the Senate House in the direction of Gonville and Caius, his gait as clipped and precise as his speech.

'What was all that about?' Gloria asked.

'I really don't know.'

'Is he always so abrupt?'

'I've never seen him behave like that before. Very odd.' As the tutor disappeared into the distance, George took his wife's arm. 'We'd better get moving,' he said, 'if we're going to get your trunks down from Girton before five.'

'Hang on a minute,' Gloria said, darting back to where the results were displayed. 'I haven't looked at what Lionel got!'

It took an hour of manoeuvring to get the larger of Gloria's two trunks up the narrow stairs to their flat on Botolph Lane.

George's face was flushed red, Lionel's bathed in sweat, as they finally set it down in the middle of the tiny living room. Gloria handed each of them a large glass of cold water.

'There's just the one with the books left now,' she said brightly. George and Lionel groaned in unison. 'We left it sticking out through the door at the bottom of the stairs onto the pavement. We can't leave it there much longer.'

George, draining his glass, stood up wearily. 'I tell you what, Lionel. You stand by the window and I'll throw up the heavier books to you one by one. Then maybe we can carry it up those stairs without breaking our blooming backs.' Lionel, still panting, lifted a hand in acknowledgement as George disappeared out the door.

'I'm sorry about your two-two, Lionel,' Gloria said as she took the glasses back to the tiny kitchen. 'I thought you would have done far better.'

'Not all of us get first-class honours, battleship. I had to work quite hard for my result too, you know. A matter of fine judgement!'

'You didn't . . .' Gloria said suspiciously, emerging to study Lionel's face. 'You did! You deliberately did badly in the exams!'

'A matter of survival, my dear,' Lionel replied, producing a large silk handkerchief and mopping his brow. 'Man, my mother wrote me the most terrifying letter a few months ago. All about how the aged parent is ready to retire and leave his empire for his fine young son to run. As soon as I am well qualified, she said, I must return to Guyana.'

'But that sounds wonderful.'

'In time. All in good time.' Lionel strolled over to the window and looked out. 'I thought another year walking the hallowed halls wouldn't do me any harm.' He turned and grinned at Gloria, stuffing his handkerchief back into his breast-pocket. 'And if the old lion loses a few more teeth while I am gone, all the better.'

'You just don't want to grow up, Lionel Ramkissoon,' Gloria accused.

'*Au contraire, mon enfant*,' he remonstrated. 'I know exactly what growing up entails and I intend to put it off as long as I possibly can.'

'Lionel!' George shouted beneath the window. 'Friendly fire!' A large textbook sailed briskly through the living-room window. Lionel dove for it like a wicket-keeper, rolling to his feet with the book in hand.

'How could I leave,' he demanded, catching the next tome as it sailed through the window, 'when I am obviously needed here to be of aid and succour to my friends!' When no other book was forthcoming, he peered out of the window. 'Fire when ready!' A slim volume sailed viciously past his left ear.

'Don't worry about us,' Gloria laughed. 'We'll survive!'

Dr Weekes stood gazing out of his study window across the courtyard of Gonville and Caius. Behind him, Gloria and George sat side by side on his sofa. Dr Weekes turned and looked at them for a moment through narrowed eyes.

'Don't get too settled on that sofa, George,' he said. 'I need you to go to the Porter's Lodge for me. I am expecting a parcel to be delivered there.'

George looked surprised. 'Right.'

'Now, laddie.'

'Yes, Dr Weekes.'

As the door closed behind him, Dr Weekes turned to face Gloria. 'I'm afraid this was all a bit of a ruse, my dear. It is you to whom I wish to speak.' He was standing over where she sat on the sofa and for a moment Gloria felt afraid.

'Me? But . . .'

Abruptly, Dr Weekes sat down opposite her, smiled at her.

'May I say congratulations on your first. Well done. Well done indeed.'

'Thank you.'

'It seems to me,' he continued thoughtfully, 'that you have had your chance at getting the education you want. Coming to Cambridge is a privilege that some people do not fully appreciate.' He looked directly at her as he said this.

'I worked extremely hard to get here, Dr Weekes,' Gloria stated.

'So did your husband.'

'I know that,' she agreed warily. What was he getting at? The tutor spent another moment or two looking at her before getting up and going to stand once again by his window.

'You have to understand that I teach here, year in, year out. I see a parade of young men of varying ability pass through this university. There are,' he said, turning to face her, 'those whose fathers and grandfathers came to Cambridge and who see this as some sort of grown-up boarding school and me as the house-master. There are those who have worked terribly hard to be here and who beaver away, day in and day out, without ever having a single original thought in their heads.' He paused, and pulling his pince-nez from his waistcoat pocket, balanced them on the bridge of his nose to peer at Gloria more closely. 'And then there are those odd, shining individuals who actually make this job a joy. Like George.' He slid the pince-nez back into their pocket and spoke venomously. 'I am telling you this, Mrs Compton, because I want you to know that I shall hold you personally responsible if George ruins his chances in this life.'

'I beg your pardon?'

'When the brightest undergraduate I have had in years stands to risk his academic success in order to meet responsibilities you had no right forcing on him!' Dr Weekes spat.

'Forcing on him!' Gloria interrupted him indignantly. But before she could say more:

'And as for getting married without letting the college know what he was planning to do – he could have been sent down, his whole future compromised!'

'We felt it was worth the risk,' Gloria stated, fighting to stay calm.

'That damned war has promoted the most vulgar notions of the importance of romantic love,' Dr Weekes fulminated, beginning to pace up and down the length of his study. 'Love, my dear, does not conquer all. What a man like George needs is to really develop his intellectual abilities. He could have a solid,' Dr Weekes paused, then continued as if to himself, 'maybe even a brilliant, future.'

'But not if he is married to me.'

'Among the people that matter, he would always be an outsider. He would always have to work twice as hard to be acknowledged as half as good.'

'Some of us,' Gloria said in a voice from which she struggled to exclude bitterness, 'have lived with that all our lives.'

Dr Weekes stopped pacing and came again to sit directly opposite her. 'Exactly. And is that something you would wish on George?'

The words, thrown as accurately as darts, stung her.

'No,' she whispered. 'No, it isn't.' Taking a deep breath and pulling herself up straight, Gloria looked directly at Dr Weeks. 'Why are you telling me all this?'

'Because he is so in love with you he can't see straight,' the man explained. 'Because at least one of you ought to view the situation without rose-tinted spectacles. Do you want to be responsible for holding him back in this life?'

'You don't know me, Dr Weekes, if you think that for one moment I would allow myself to be a burden to him!'

When George re-entered his tutor's study, he found Gloria sitting bolt upright and Dr Weekes walking towards the table in the corner where a small decanter and three glasses were standing.

'The porter said you picked up the package this morning, Dr Weekes,' George said, glancing at Gloria.

'Did I?' Dr Weekes poured sherry into the glasses. 'How forgetful I am becoming. Do sit and try some of this sherry, George. I think you'll be amused . . .' he shot a glance over at Gloria '. . . by its presumption.'

'You're very quiet,' George remarked later as they entered the flat on Botolph Lane. The summer-evening sunshine filled the room with a soft light that made even the mottled walls look presentable. George crossed to the window over the Lane and opened it, letting in the sound of laughter and conversations from Trumpington Street a hundred yards away. 'Very quiet indeed.'

'Am I?' Gloria asked listlessly. She sat on the larger of her two trunks and looked around the room.

'I thought you would want to celebrate your results.'

'It's funny. The first thing I wanted to do was sit down and write a letter home.'

'Why don't you? I'm sure they'll be delighted.'

Gloria shook her head. 'I'm probably the last person they want to hear from. I'm on my own, remember?'

George came and sat beside her on the trunk. 'No, my love. We are in this together.' He gave her shoulders a quick squeeze. 'Now,' he said briskly, 'shall I take your jacket? That's one thing we have plenty of in this place: pegs to hang coats on.' She wriggled out of the jacket and he went to hang it by the door.

'Haven't you ever wondered if we did the right thing?' Gloria asked. 'If we should have got married, if you should be cutting your studies short . . .'

'No, I don't wonder,' George said, coming to kneel in front of her.

'Dr Weekes said you could have a great future.' Gloria touched his face gently.

'We won't always live like this, my love. I'll make damn sure of that.' He handed her an envelope. 'It was in the pocket of your jacket.' Gloria took it but put it down on the trunk beside her. 'Well?' George asked. 'Aren't you going to open it?'

'It's from Jamaica. It's probably just Mother reminding me how ungrateful I am. She will probably call you "this young man" at least three times and I don't have the strength for it right now.' She reached up and cupped his face again, her eyes full of tenderness.

'You have been in the oddest mood ever since we got back,' he said, frowning. 'Did Weekes say something to upset you?'

Gloria gave a sharp bark of laughter. 'He couldn't upset me if he tried. Now, let's see what old Albertha Theodocia Carter has to say to me!' She grabbed the letter and ripped it open unceremoniously. A quick read and, for the first time, her face was wreathed by a smile of genuine happiness.

'Care to share it?' George asked.

'It's not from Mother. It's from Father. "*Dear Gloria, Fifteen pounds enclosed. Wedding present. Your mother upset and sulking. Will deny sending you this if asked. Suggest you do same. Father.*" '

'Good man,' George laughed.

'The best,' Gloria agreed. 'It's nice to feel there's someone on my side after all.' She hugged George tightly. 'Maybe I will survive all this.'

'We both will, my love,' he promised. 'We both will. Now, what shall we spend it on? A dining table?' he asked, looking around the empty flat.

'No,' Gloria disagreed. 'A desk. For you.'

'I feel,' he said, 'almost affluent! Put your jacket on again, love. Time to go and celebrate!'

As they left the flat, George pulled the door closed behind them and stopped at the top of the stairs. Gloria, halfway down, looked back to see him standing with a broad smile on his face. 'Yes,' he said, 'definitely a day to celebrate. I like my new father-in-law already!'

'Pull harder, Lionel!'

Swathed in an oversize apron, her hair tucked under a scarf, Gloria stood in the kitchen tugging mightily on the skin that still covered the front legs of a rabbit. Lionel, a look of utter distaste on his face, was holding onto the skinned back legs.

'I wish I could! These back legs keep slipping through my hands,' he complained.

'I have,' Gloria said, 'to get,' tugging harder, 'these stupid rabbits skinned, so keep pulling. When George decided to invite Dr Weekes to dinner, I promised him we would have jugged hare – and jugged hare . . .' she heaved mightily '. . . we shall have!'

It was October, 1946, and the couple had been living in Botolph Lane for three months now.

'This from the woman who refused to mend my shirts?' Lionel asked.

'I'm married to George, remember?' Gloria asked, breathless with the effort. 'I'm trying to be a good wife.' With a ripping, sucking sound, the skin of the rabbit finally gave way. Letting go the hindquarters, Lionel sprang back, whipping out a large yellow handkerchief. He wiped minute blood and fat stains from his immaculate, primrose-yellow shirt.

'Disgusting,' he concluded. 'Don't you think you should have had them skinned and gutted before bringing them home, battleship?'

'I hate cooking.' Gloria looked despairingly at the two other rabbits that lay stiff on the table waiting to be skinned.

Putting his handkerchief over his nose, Lionel retired from the kitchen. 'Take a deep breath and start cleaning, my good woman,' he advised from the comfort of the living room. 'Jugged hare, remember!'

'When I was a little girl,' Gloria said, as she set to work on the second rabbit, 'I never questioned where dinner came from. We went to the table and there it was. Roast pork. Rice and peas . . .'

'Curry mutton and roti,' Lionel said nostalgically.

'Sweet St Vincent yam roasted on an open fire. And mangoes so ripe you got juice all down your blouse when you bit into them.'

When Lionel put his head around the kitchen door, Gloria was standing over the sink, staring into the middle distance, a dreamy smile on her face. He stood for a moment, watching her, before he spoke.

'I think you'd better go on cleaning that rabbit before it gets so gamy it walks out of this kitchen all by itself.'

'I hope George appreciates what I do for him,' Gloria said, falling to her task again.

'I hope,' Lionel muttered, 'he appreciates what you've given up for him.'

'I haven't given anything up,' Gloria snapped, giving him a hard look.

'Where would you be right now, if you weren't here?' Lionel asked softly.

'But I am here!' Gloria thought her voice sounded too loud, too defensive, even in her own head.

'Answer the question.'

'Why should I? It's a nonsense question. I'm not in Jamaica. I am here. With my husband. Trying to make dinner.' She turned to face Lionel. 'And if you ever dare mention to George that I had a clerkship with one of Jamaica's leading law firms within my grasp . . .' Lionel put his hands up in mock surrender '. . . or my mother's cooking . . .' Lionel put his finger over his lips ' . . . or anything . . .'

'*Moi?*' he asked, all injured innocence. '*Jamais de ma vie!* Besides, I don't need to mention them, do I?'

'I am married to George,' Gloria said, turning back to her rabbits. 'I have to try and make our life together the best it can be. And I will,' she insisted. 'You'll see.'

'That was,' Dr Weekes said, leaning back in his chair and dabbing at his lips with his napkin, 'the best meal I have had in weeks, Gloria. And rabbit is not among my favourite fare. Well done.'

George beamed. Lionel glanced at Gloria who was looking flustered but pleased. 'She laboured long and hard over it, didn't you, Gloria?' Lionel prompted.

'I was happy to do it.'

'It seems to me,' George resumed the discussion they had been having, 'that if the colonies do become independent, they might better be able to tailor their production to the needs of their own populations, rather than the imperial super-economy.'

Dr Weekes shook his head with certainty. 'Economies of scale, my boy,' he stated. 'Raw materials in and of themselves have no value until processed and sold. Africa may produce the rubber and iron and cocoa that keeps our industries fed, but it cannot, in and of itself, add that value to its own raw materials. No, the colonies,' he concluded, 'need Britain.'

'More than Britain needs the colonies?' Lionel asked, his voice so intense that even Gloria glanced nervously across at him. 'If there were no raw materials, surely there would be no industry?'

'You can always find another source of raw materials, my boy,' Dr Weekes said.

'Maybe what the colonies need is to find a new, more equitable system into which to feed their products,' Lionel pointed out, '*my boy*.'

Dr Weekes's eyebrows flew up; George froze; Gloria rose and took up her plate.

'More rabbit, anyone?' she asked.

'You think that Britain exploits the colonies?' George asked Lionel.

'It does seem to me that Britain would not have survived the war, let alone won it, if it weren't for the generosity of the colonies past and present,' Lionel replied.

'At least,' Dr Weekes interrupted, 'we won the war!'

'Dessert, anyone?' Gloria asked in despairing tones.

'At what price? That is the question,' Lionel retorted.

'Dr Weekes – dessert?' George asked.

'What?' the tutor barked.

'*Dessert.*'

'Yes!' he snapped, then relented. 'Yes, please.'

'Lionel? Dessert?' Gloria asked.

'Of course.'

Piling the dishes and cutlery on top of his own, George carried them into the kitchen, leaving Gloria to struggle to break what was a palpable silence around the table.

'Maybe we should find something rather less contentious to talk about, Dr Weekes,' she suggested.

'Absolutely, my dear,' he agreed, too heartily. 'After all, you are married to an Englishman now. We don't want you having divided loyalties, do we?' Gloria ignored Lionel's flashing glance. 'How have you and the in-laws taken to each other? Well, I hope?' Dr Weekes ventured.

'I haven't actually met them yet, Dr Weekes,' Gloria explained. 'George has been working very hard recently.'

'But we're going to go and visit soon,' George announced, entering with a large tray laden with dessert paraphernalia.

'Are we?' Gloria asked. Lionel looked keenly from her face to her husband's.

'Of course. I'm sure they'll take to Gloria like a duck to water,' George said.

Lionel could not contain a snort of laughter. 'It should be . . . interesting,' he agreed, choosing his words.

'Very interesting,' Dr Weekes nodded, looking eagerly at the fragrant dish George was setting in the middle of the table. 'Is that peach cobbler I smell, by any chance?'

CHAPTER TWELVE

THE GLEAMING WATERS of the Trent lapped against the stone steps where the graveyard sloped down to meet the riverbank. Sitting side by side on a bench, Gloria and George watched a pair of swans glide along the edge of the river, occasionally dipping long necks into its green waters.

'Ha'pennyworth of sweets and a good book, was it?' Gloria asked.

'Every Saturday morning of my school life,' George confirmed. 'First the library for the book, the market for the sweets and then spending the rest of the day here reading. I knew if I went home, my father would have pots for me to wash, flowerbeds for me to weed. This was much better.'

'Don't you think it's time we faced it?' Gloria asked, stroking a strand of dark brown hair off his face.

'Are you absolutely sure you want to do this?' he said.

'We might as well get it over with. We can't come all the way to Burton-on-Trent and not see where you grew up, at the very least.'

'The towering oasthouses? The sweet smell of hops in the wind? Perhaps you'll be impressed by the majestic presence of the Branston pickle factory?'

Gloria grinned, taking his arm as they walked along the Trent to where a side street led them to the centre of Burton.

Their route took them over the water meadows on a wrought-iron footbridge. George stopped when they were halfway across.

'I skived off under this bridge during many a school cross-country run, my dear. Ah, youth.' He smiled at his wife then looked over her shoulder to where the rows of terraced houses rose rank on rank beyond the water meadows' edge.

'You know we had to come,' Gloria said. 'I couldn't avoid meeting your mother for ever.'

'Yes,' he agreed, nodded and set off towards the houses. 'We had to come.'

'Don't look now, but just about every lace curtain in the street is twitching,' George whispered as they walked along his street. 'This is it,' he said as they arrived at a door painted blue, the brass knocker buffed to gold. Curious children appeared in several of the doorways as they passed. The blue door opened almost before George had finished knocking.

'I'm surprised you had the cheek to come here,' Mrs Compton spat at them as she pulled them into her hallway, snapping the door shut behind them.

'Hello, Mum,' George said.

'Half the street is staring at the pair of you. And your busybody Aunt Anne will be telling anybody who missed the sight exactly what she saw!'

'Mum, this is Gloria,' George began.

'I'm well aware who she is, thank you very much!' Mrs Compton said tightly, glaring at Gloria. 'Wipe your feet!'

'I asked him to bring me, Mrs Compton,' Gloria said, feeling confined by the small hallway and her mother-in-law's patent loathing.

'Did you? And what exactly did you think you would accomplish by that?'

'I thought we ought to get to know each other.'

'Why?' Mrs Compton looked bitterly at George. 'My son made it quite clear that he had no intention of considering my feelings when he decided to ditch the nice girl he was engaged to for three years . . .' George looked pleadingly at Gloria '. . . the girl who has been friend and comfort to me all the time he was away fighting, the girl who is still . . .' she faced George accusingly, 'heartbroken. He didn't consider my feelings then!'

George, who had been in the middle of taking Gloria's coat, pulled it back on over her shoulders, and reached for the door. His face was ashen with contained rage. Before he could open it, Gloria stopped him and turned back to face the small woman who smelled of soap and brass polish and who stood, her narrow face pinched with resentment, filling the hall with her anger.

'He is your son.'

'And my only child. My only child – and look at what he's done!' Again Gloria stopped George from opening the front door. 'Made me the laughing stock of the street I've lived on all my life.' She imitated a jeering voice. ' "Look at Ethel Compton – her son went to the grammar school and got himself a scholarship to Cambridge and then went and married some *coloured* girl. Popped back to tell his fiancée he couldn't marry her and then buggered off!" '

'I tried to explain it to you. You wouldn't listen!' The words burst out of George.

'I'm glad your father is dead,' Mrs Compton hissed at her son. 'I'm glad he doesn't have to see this.'

George fought for control. He shook as if with ague when he turned to Gloria and spoke in a voice so low she could barely hear it.

'Let's go.'

'Would you want George to marry someone he didn't love? Would you want him to be unhappy?' Gloria cried, appealing to the woman who stood, arms crossed on her chest, face frozen with scorn.

'You marry,' she replied slowly, as if she were instructing a fool, 'someone like yourself, someone who understands you and where you come from. What do you know about people like us? What do you know about George?'

'She knows everything about me, Mum. She knows more about me than you will ever know.' George took Gloria's hand and opened the front door. 'I'm sorry you don't want to be part of our lives. At least we tried.'

As they stepped out into the street, Mrs Compton snatched wide the door.

'It's all roses and romance now,' she shouted. 'But you'll live to regret it, mark my words.'

'I regret bringing Gloria here,' George replied. 'That is the only thing I regret.'

'Mrs Compton, there must be some way ...?' Gloria began, aware that the street was suddenly full of people listening to them with keen attention.

'Of course there is a way,' the woman said, playing to her growing audience. 'Leave him. Leave us alone. Let him get on with his life.' She retreated inside, slamming the door heavily behind her. A few people in the crowd applauded.

'Just goes to show,' remarked one woman to another, 'what happens when you rise above your station in life.' There were murmurs of agreement. George began to push his way through the crush, pulling Gloria behind him.

'Don't give them the satisfaction of seeing you are upset,' he told her.

'But some of them are following us, George!'

He looked back to see a dozen or so children, egged on by laughing parents, following them back along the street towards the bridge. One boy, bolder than the rest, ran up to George.

'Where'd you find her, George Compton? Down the pits?' he called and was rewarded by hoots of laughter from his companions. Gloria tightened her grip on George's arm to stop him from going after the miscreant.

They lost the last of their tormentors about halfway across the bridge. In the house at the end of the row, a plump, red-haired woman lit a cigarette off the butt she had been balancing in the corner of her mouth and inhaled heavily. Through a veil of smoke, she watched as the couple walked away from her street, noticed how the young woman stroked the hair from the young man's forehead as they went, and shook her head.

Lionel lounged across the arrangement of cushions that passed for a couch in the Comptons' living room, examining his boots for signs of scuffing. Gloria, wearing three sweaters and a pair of George's wool socks over her wool tights, sat opposite him, nursing a cup of hot, weak tea.

'I think it is the first time that I have felt really . . . really hated,' she confessed. 'I thought they were going to attack us. I have never seen George so angry.'

'Speaking of whom, where is that prince among men?' Lionel enquired. 'I know he isn't here because the fire is out and somehow it never is when his lordship is at home.'

'At the library,' Gloria replied, ignoring his taunt with dignity. 'On our budget, he can't afford some of the texts, I'm afraid, and as he has to go to two sets of lectures, he prefers to study there in-between.'

'What about you? No luck finding work?'

'I nearly got one at the glove counter at Ryder & Lilley,' Gloria said, 'but they decided they needed someone with more . . . experience.' She smiled ruefully. 'With all the men coming home, what jobs there are, are going fast.'

'Mind you, sometimes,' Lionel said pensively, 'that blunt prejudice of the working class is easier to cope with than all the mealy-mouthed "we are all equal in God's eyes" pap.

I have to admit that one of my favourite pastimes is eating in the most expensive resturant I can find and watching the faces of my fellow diners. "Didn't we leave the wogs in the Punjab, old chap?" is printed very boldly across their foreheads. Although of course they say nothing. And the waiters are often exquisitely polite.'

'It is,' Gloria reminded him, 'a little different when you are rich, Lionel.'

'Still no sign of a thaw on the home front?' he asked.

'Oh, one brief letter from Mother to inform me that she had put an announcement of our marriage in the *Gleaner* to stop people from gossiping, and that she hadn't had the heart to tell Mr Ashenheim that I had turned my back on his offer of a job. And that the doctor had said she was suffering from nerves.'

'And of course you have not written to apologize?' Lionel enquired.

'Why should I?' Gloria demanded. 'Is it such a terrible thing for me to want to be happy?'

'Cease fire, battleship! I am not the enemy!'

'It just makes me so angry,' Gloria sighed. 'All we did was get married.'

'Is it?' Lionel asked, one eyebrow arched.

'Don't,' Gloria countered and was startled by a loud knock on the door.

Lionel leapt to his feet.

'That must be my surprise,' he said.

Gloria shook her head despairingly. 'If you are trying to drag me into another one of your schemes . . .'

'Now now,' Lionel chided as he opened the door, 'just because I have a taste for frivolity doesn't mean there isn't a serious side to my character.'

A tall, sturdy man with an open face and observant eyes entered the flat, ducking a little to get through the front door.

'Gloria, this is Harry. Harry, Gloria.'

'Pleased to meet you, Harry,' Gloria said, looking to Lionel for an explanation.

'Likewise,' Harry replied. 'You don't mind if I put these things down, do you? Just my training kit,' he explained, and stowed a muddy canvas bag behind the door.

'You see, Gloria dear, Harry here is American. He started studying for his LLB this year.'

'Not terribly successfully, I'm afraid,' Harry said sheepishly.

'And he is in the University boat,' Lionel continued. 'The thing is that Harry needs help. Like you, he needs to make the transition from North American to British education. I imagine his Greek requires some polishing, and you know how offended our lecturers get if you are not *au fait* with their latest brilliant piece of legal analysis.'

'Lionel said that you were the smartest person he knew and he thought you might be able to help me,' Harry concluded.

'For a modest fee, of course. By the hour. Here in the flat,' Lionel clarified.

Gloria looked dubiously from one eager face to the other.

'I can't tell you how much I would appreciate this, Gloria,' Harry confided. 'The thing is, I brought my wife and baby son over with me. Love them to death, but there isn't much work I can get done at home. Besides training on the river at all hours, I need somewhere in town I can study.'

'Harry,' Lionel confirmed, 'is very serious about his rowing.'

'Hell, yes. We're going to whup Oxford but good this year!'

'So what do you say, my love?' Lionel enquired.

'Yes,' Gloria heard herself saying. 'Yes, of course. Delighted.' Her fingers were immediately lost in Harry's huge grip as he shook her hand.

'I thought you might,' said Lionel, looking pleased with himself. 'What did I say, Harry?'

'You said if anybody could get me through these exams, Mrs Gloria Compton could,' the big American grinned, still pumping Gloria's arm energetically.

'That's exactly what I said,' Lionel beamed. 'I tell you what, Harry, why don't I meet you downstairs?'

'Sure thing,' Harry agreed immediately. Gloria realized his bluff geniality hid a sharp mind. 'Nice meeting you, Gloria.'

As soon as the door closed behind him, Lionel turned to Gloria, buffing his nails on the lapel of his coat.

'Nice boy, Harry. Rich as Croesus. Not a malicious bone in his body. Lionel done good?' he enquired.

'He done very good,' Gloria nodded.

'Good lord,' Lionel said in surprise as he opened the door, 'I think I feel almost virtuous!'

'No.'

'But I already told Harry I *would* tutor him,' Gloria stated, placing George's dinner in front of him where he sat at their small dining table.

'Without consulting me?' he asked. He pushed the fatty stew around on the plate with his fork.

'We need the money, darling! What's the point of my sitting around here all day when I could be earning?'

'I thought,' George said stiffly, radiating offended dignity, 'we had worked out how we could manage.' He pushed his plate away, closing the knife and fork with finality.

'We'll freeze to death in winter and starve to death all year.'

'Did Lionel have anything to do with this?' George asked.

Gloria paused before replying. 'Does it matter?' she asked, taking up his plate and heading for the kitchen.

'Yes, damn it, it does. How do you think it makes me feel to be bailed out by one of your wealthy West Indian friends?

Lionel seems to think that we are his pet project and should always be grateful to him.'

'He doesn't think anything of the kind!' Gloria emerged from the kitchen to sit opposite George at the table, her face troubled.

'Then why is he always around?' George demanded. 'Why is he always trying to play the fairy godfather?'

'We really do live in different worlds, don't we,' Gloria sighed. She got up from the table and went to stand by the window looking down on the Lane.

'I asked you a question – you can't answer it. Don't retreat into that kind of attitude just because you can't answer it.'

'Oh,' Gloria said, turning back to face him, 'I can answer. I'm just not sure you are ready to hear it.'

'I fought in the bloody war, for God's sake. I don't think there is too much I haven't seen or can't handle!'

Gloria came slowly to sit opposite him again, her eyes never leaving his face.

'Lionel knows what I know, George,' she began. 'He knows that no matter how polite people are, no matter how friendly they seem, they don't want us here. Every day we get up and put on a second skin, a defence against every glance, every half-heard, muttered phrase, every falsely bright smile. And we help each other out. Lionel knows, just like I do, that I am never going to find a decent job.'

George opened his mouth to protest but Gloria put up her hand to stop him. 'So he finds a way for me to earn. In exchange, he has a place – here, George – where he can come where it doesn't matter what colour he is, or what his nationality is. He truly is welcome.'

George looked down, unable to meet that bright gaze, those direct eyes. 'I'm sorry about what happened in Burton, my love,' he said, 'but you can't tar everyone with the same brush.'

Gloria's eyebrows shot up at the inept metaphor. George flushed scarlet.

'It won't always be like this!' he exploded.

'Won't it?' Gloria asked with a look of pity on her face. 'Why do you think people are so angry with you for marrying me?'

'They don't know you,' George protested.

'They don't know who I am, but they know what I am,' she corrected him.

'So is that it?' George demanded. 'Is your colour going to dominate our whole marriage?' Is our whole life from now on going to be about our differences?'

'Not here,' Gloria said. 'Not within our home. But out there? Yes, probably.'

'You are my bride.' George's voice ached with emotion. 'You are married to me. I should be the one making things right. I should be the one who can support us. Not Lionel!'

'And you know I would go barking mad if all I did was sit around here all day,' Gloria said, struggling to smile. 'I'm sorry I said I would tutor Harry without discussing it with you first.'

George too smiled, though his face was still tight with frustration. 'Never tell Lionel what I said about him,' he pleaded.

'I don't think he would mind in the slightest,' Gloria replied. 'But I won't tell him,' she continued soothingly.

'I'm absolutely exhausted,' George admitted. 'Dr Weekes is really pushing me.'

'Maybe he wants you to change your mind, stop trying to do everything in one year.'

'Snowball's chance in hell and he knows it. And if you give me that "are you sure?" look one more time, I'll . . .' George got up and began to walk around the table towards her.

'What will you do?' Gloria asked, eluding him. '*Mmm?*'

'Come over here and I'll show you exactly what I'll do!'

Radnor   *28th November 1946*
Half Way Tree Post Office
St Andrew

Dear Gloria,

I am writing to you because Father says I must. It seems that your husband wrote him and ever since he read the letter, he has been very unkind to me. He says that I judged this young man without even giving him a chance, and that all I was interested in was arranging a large wedding to impress people like Mrs Marley. He has never spoken to me like that before! So far I have not been able to find the letter to read it for myself, so I don't know exactly what your husband said. Yet.

More out of habit than anything else, I have made up and will send off a parcel to you. Mrs Thompson says that no end to the shortages is in sight. I am sending her one as well, as she has been a good friend to me: guava cheese, mango jam and some tamarind balls Cook insisted on putting in because you liked them as a girl.

Congratulations on your first-class honours. It was of course what we expected but perhaps congratulations are due anyway. Father says you are shortly to be called to the Bar at Gray's Inn. Please write and let him know as soon as you get the confirmation instead of waiting for months to tell him like with your exam results.

Mother

Gloria looked up from where she was coaxing a few lumps of coke to burn in the grate and smiled at Harry who sat, surrounded by a maelstrom of paper, at her dining table.

'I thought you argued it very well, Harry,' she said, pulling her heavy sweater closer around her. 'I just wondered if you wouldn't get your ideas across more forcefully if you wrote in the active voice, rather than the passive.'

'I think you actually praised my work there, Gloria. Be

careful now,' he grinned. 'It might just go to my head. I'm not used to it.'

Gloria stood, brushing the coke-dust off her hands, to answer a soft knock at the door.

'Why don't you look through the first couple of paragraphs and change the voice and see what difference it makes,' she suggested as she opened the door.

'Margaret! How lovely to see you!' Gloria recognized Jimmy immediately from the photograph Margaret had carried in her wallet all through the war. He leaned heavily on his cane as they entered the flat and Gloria couldn't help noticing how much older her friend looked than when she had last seen her. With all four of them inside, the flat felt full to bursting.

'I won't offer to take your coats,' Gloria told them. 'The only difference between inside here and outside is that there aren't any draughts in here!'

'Gloria, this is Jimmy,' Margaret said.

'Nice to finally meet you, Jimmy. I feel as though we are old friends.'

'I'm sorry to drop in on you like this. It was a spur-of-the-moment decision, wasn't it, Jimmy?' Margaret began but he had drifted over to the window and stood looking down on the street below. 'We can come back later when you're not busy,' she said, flustered.

'The thing is, Gloria,' Harry said, standing and gathering some of his papers into a pile, 'I'm kinda anxious to get home today. The wife's due to have our second baby and I'd like to know if it's arrived yet. If you don't mind?'

'Go!' Gloria commanded him, laughing. 'Go! Immediately!'

'I'm hoping it's a boy!' Harry called over his shoulder as he ducked through the doorway and clattered down the stairs.

'Well, you've made the flat look quite nice,' Margaret volunteered, looking around her.

'If you can pretend George's books and papers aren't scattered everywhere,' Gloria replied, clearing a space for the couple on the makeshift couch. 'So tell me everything. How is your course going? When are you two getting married?'

'That's what I keep asking her, Gloria,' Jimmy spoke up. He came to join them from the window.

'You know your leg hasn't healed fully yet, dear. And I still have to finish studying for my teaching certificate,' Margaret said, taking his hand and stroking it. Jimmy pulled it away.

'I still don't see why that should stop us from getting married, Meg.' He buttoned up his coat and wrapped his scarf around his cheeks. 'You talk some sense into her, Gloria. I'm going to go take a look around this town I've heard so much about.'

'What time will you be back?' Margaret called after his retreating figure, but the door clicked shut behind him without sound of an answer. Margaret took to examining her nails with minute attention.

'Is everything all right?' Gloria asked after a moment.

'He's gone,' her friend said in tones of disgust, 'for a drink. He always does. He thinks I don't know about it, but I do. And I hate it.'

'I'm so sorry.'

'Why should you be?' Margaret asked, her voice suddenly hard, brittle. 'At least he came back alive. I should be grateful for that. I should be happy.'

'But you aren't, are you?'

'It was so much better when we were writing to each other. I had my life and he had his and we just loved each other because we wanted to.' Margaret's voice quavered then broke.

'Oh, God. That sounds so awful, as if I think the war was a good thing. I still care for him. I always will . . .'

'But is it enough?' Gloria asked.

'You see?' Margaret fought to smile at her friend. 'That's why I came. You were never afraid of the hard questions. I don't know, Gloria! I don't know if it is enough. I don't know if I am strong enough to do this.'

'And what does Jimmy say?'

'He calls me Meg and he hugs me and gives me a little smile.' Margaret whispered, 'and then he goes out again. I don't know what he thinks any more; I don't know what he wants. Today, I asked him what he wanted to do, where he wanted to go. "Wherever you want, Meg. Whatever you want to do." It's as if he's hollow inside.'

'That picture you kept in your wallet didn't do him justice. He is so handsome,' Gloria said, trying to rally her.

'That's my Jimmy,' Margaret agreed. 'So handsome.'

'You are both going to stay for dinner, of course?'

'We couldn't impose—' Margaret began but Gloria cut her off with a chuckle.

'You have a choice of Meat and Veg or Spam, I'm afraid. Hardly an imposition. More like a shared hardship.'

'That really was quite good,' Margaret declared bravely as she closed her knife and fork.

'No, it wasn't,' Gloria said, getting up and gathering their plates for clearing. 'But it was edible, I suppose. Jimmy, you didn't eat much.'

'He never does, do you, Jimmy? You prefer other kinds of nourishment,' Margaret said sourly, getting up from the table to help Gloria.

'Don't start on me, Meg. I'm a grown man.'

'Shall I wash and you dry, or do you prefer to wash, Gloria?' Margaret enquired, ignoring him.

'I'll do them later. Come and have some coffee. Mother relented enough to send me a couple of pounds and I've been making it stretch.'

When Gloria emerged from the kitchen with the three cups of coffee, Jimmy was again standing by the window, peering out through the frost that was creeping up the panes. Margaret sat curled up among the cushions.

'I'm sorry George couldn't be here tonight,' Gloria said.

'If he has to study, he has to study. I completely understand.'

'I wish I did,' Gloria said, sipping gingerly at the scalding, black liquid.

Margaret fanned the steam from the cup towards her face, revelling in the warmth and aroma of it. 'Has he been studying a lot lately?' she asked.

'He has to, I know that,' Gloria replied. 'But sometimes . . .'

'Spit it out, dear,' Margaret advised.

'Sometimes, I think he prefers to be in the college library than here. He just seems to spend more and more time there.'

'I was so caught up in my own trouble, I never even thought to ask.' Margaret's concern for her friend drove the petulant look from her face. 'Is everything all right between the pair of you?'

'Yes, I think so.' Gloria shrugged and sighed. 'He just sets these impossibly high standards for himself and then gets so angry when he can't do everything perfectly. He thinks he should be able to do two years' academic work in one, support us, look after me . . .'

Margaret smiled with genuine amusement for the first time since she'd arrived. She did not notice Jimmy slipping out of the front door, closing it quietly behind him.

'*Look after you?*'

'It's not funny,' Gloria chided her.

'It is, a bit. How can you accuse George of being a perfectionist when that is exactly what you are, too?'

'I am not!'

'Afraid you might be less than perfect if you admit to it?' Margaret teased.

'Some friend you are,' Gloria rallied and looked to Jimmy for support. 'Margaret, where's your man?' she asked and watched the veil of bitterness fall over her friend's face.

'Where do you think? And I didn't even hear him leave this time.'

'Shall we go and find him?' Gloria suggested.

'Why bother? He'll be back when he's had a skinful. He always is!'

Gloria tiptoed across the cold floor into the bedroom, carrying the old hot-water bottle as if it were a gift from the gods. She stowed it in her side of the bed and leapt in, pulling the covers up to her chin. George watched her in some amusement then climbed in beside her.

'I wish,' she said as he settled in beside her, 'that you could have been here this evening.'

'I can't be in two places at one time, love,' George said, reaching with his toes for the hot-water bottle.

'So be here then,' Gloria said, pushing his feet away. 'Just once in a while be here! Margaret was so concerned about Jimmy wandering off that I was beginning to get really worried.'

'He came back, didn't he?' George yawned. 'He probably got tired of listening to you two reminiscing about your days at Girton.'

'Every time I looked at him, I got this odd feeling that he didn't care how much longer he lived. I think Margaret sees it too.'

'Maybe,' George murmured, 'it's for the best.'

'George!' Gloria sat bolt upright in bed, letting in a huge draught of cold air.

George hauled her back down and wrapped both of them in the blankets. 'Some men never recover from the war, love,' he said, pulling her close. 'There was this one man in our division when I was in North Africa, came to us after the rest of his division had been wiped out. It took him two months to die. He just faded away. He didn't want to live any longer.'

'One of my mother's favourite stories was about a woman who decided she was going to die when she stepped over blue powder someone had sprinkled on her doorstep. She thought she had been obeahed.'

'Obeahed?' George asked, nuzzling her neck.

'Hexed, I suppose you would call it. Obeahmen make a good living in the country parts in Jamaica. They cover everything from catching ghosts to curing infertility. Sure enough, the woman died within a month.' They lay together in silence for a few minutes, cupped like spoons.

'How is Margaret coping?' George asked.

'She does what has to be done. What else is there to do? I think she is frightened.'

'So I missed an exciting evening.'

'We missed *you*,' Gloria corrected him, pulling his arm closer around her waist.

'I'm sure you managed perfectly well without me,' George muttered, withdrawing his arm. 'After all, you're the bread-winner now, aren't you.'

Gloria turned to lie face to face, reached for his arm to place it on her body.

'I'm tried,' George said, turning away from her 'Can we talk about this some other time?'

'What's the point?'

'So,' George said drearily, 'why raise it in the first place? This is our situation. I think we should be like Margaret and just do what has to be done. *Alea iacta est*, my dear. The Rubicon is crossed and our bridges well and truly burnt. It's too late to turn back now.'

Gloria sat across from Lionel in the small restaurant and just breathed deeply. The smell of food being prepared was a real pleasure and she was determined to make the most of it. Lionel, subdued for a change in a hunter green sweater and dark suit, watched her with amusement. The waiter brought their entrée and set it down on the table without enthusiasm. Gloria, by contrast, dug in with relish.

'If I had had to eat another tin of bully beef, I think I would have thrown myself off the nearest building,' she exclaimed after savouring the first mouthful.

'Speaking of which, have you heard from the charming Margaret?' Lionel asked, taking up his fork and circling the food on his plate thoughtfully before diving in to spear a morsel.

'Last week. Still apologizing for Jimmy. This is so delicious!'

'It should be at the prices they are charging,' Lionel observed dryly. 'OK, battleship. Let's have it.'

'Have what?'

'You know exactly what I am talking about,' Lionel said. 'Every time I see George he has bags under his eyes that would make an alligator nervous.'

'He is working hard.'

'And you?' Lionel enquired, spearing another morsel.

'I'm fine,' Gloria said emphatically. 'We're both fine.'

'Fine,' mused Lionel. 'Now what exactly does that mean, I wonder? Cloudless? Tightly woven? Free from mortal illness? What, exactly?'

Gloria put down her fork and glared at him. 'What is it you want?' she demanded. 'You want me to tell you that

151

things are tense between us? That I'm scared that George is finding out what it really means to be married to a coloured woman?'

'And is he?'

'The hard way.' She paused, then: 'The third years were invited to drinks with the Master. George wasn't.'

'He isn't,' Lionel pointed out, 'a third year.'

'He is doing all the work, going to all the lectures. He should have been invited. His tutor, the despicable Dr Weekes . . .'

'I bet you don't call him that when George is around,' Lionel observed.

'. . . The devious Dr Weekes is pressuring George every which way to make him change his mind about doing two years in one.'

'He doesn't stand a chance – you know that, battleship. Hey, don't wave your fork around like that. You'll put some-one's eye out!'

'My mother,' Gloria continued after putting her fork down on her plate, 'writes me snide little letters about "this young man that you married" and he tears up any letter that comes through the door with a Burton-on-Trent postmark.'

Lionel ate for a few moments in silence, then looked up at Gloria. 'I'm afraid you can't have the silver lining without the cloud, my love,' he suggested.

'Doesn't bother me. None of it does. I'm just bloody-minded enough to enjoy proving them wrong.'

'So we return to my original question: what is it that is eating away at you so?'

'I wish you weren't so perceptive. It would be a lot easier to lie,' Gloria groaned. When Lionel answered her, his voice was so sincere, she found herself profoundly shaken. If Lionel could say such things, then the situation must be as desperate as she had schooled herself to believe it could never be.

'Do you realize,' he began, 'that for a deeply cynical creature like myself, you and George are a cause of great irritation? I hate to admit it, but I find your relationship a source of hope. And now that I have completely ruined my reputation by sinking to maudlin sentimentality, you have no choice but to respond in kind. What is it,' he said leaning forward so that his face filled her vision, 'that has the pocket battleship so frightened?'

Gloria fought to control six years of homesickness, six years of loneliness and self-doubt, six years of maintaining a carapace of competence to the world. It was several minutes before her throat relaxed enough for her to speak.

'Suppose it is all too hard, Lionel? Suppose George can't cope? I used to think that all I wanted was to be a lawyer, to have a chance to right the wrongs of this world. Sometimes I think that would be nothing compared with what I am trying to do now. Suppose I can't make our marriage work, Lionel? If I lose George, none of that would matter. Nothing would matter. That's what I'm scared of, my friend. I'm scared, after everything that's happened, after all the sacrifices we've made, I'm scared that I'm going to lose him.'

CHAPTER THIRTEEN

THROUGH THE OPEN window, the sounds of undergraduates' voices could be heard as they passed along
St Botolph's Lane below. Harry, bent over his studies at the
dining table, looked up at Gloria, his normally placid face
creased in concern.

'Maybe we should go over everything just once more.'

'Harry,' Gloria replied, hauling him to his feet, 'it has
been a pleasure tutoring you. You have made great strides,
especially once the Boat Race was over.'

'And we won,' Harry interjected. 'Don't forget, we won.'

'True – and the Cambridge Boat won. Much as I enjoy
earning the money, I can't honestly say there is anything more
I can do for you.'

The big man slowly picked up his books from the table.
'It's up to me now, I guess,' he said.

'You will be fine.'

'Darned exams aren't anything like a race, though. I can't
just pull harder, if you see what I mean. If I was just a little
more certain that I had covered everything . . .'

'You have,' Gloria assured him, handing him the books
he hadn't yet picked up. 'Everything – I promise. Harry, trust
me. You are ready for these exams!' He continued to look
dubious. 'It is a beautiful spring day. Go and take your wife
for tea at Grantchester, take your children punting on the
Cam, go and *enjoy yourself* – so that when you get into that
exam room tomorrow, you'll be relaxed and ready to write.'

Harry shrugged and smiled then headed for the door. He turned back as he opened it, a small package in one hand.

'I wanted you to have this,' he said, suddenly shy. 'To say thank you for allowing me to track mud in here after training and for being so patient.' He had obviously rehearsed the speech and ran out of breath just before the end. He thrust the package at her. Opening it, Gloria found a gleaming pen nestling in a velvet-lined case.

'Gold nib. Should last you a while.'

'Thank you, Harry,' Gloria said, delightedly turning it over in her hands. Her initials G. C. C. were engraved on the side. 'It is really lovely.'

'I hope you don't mind, but I told a couple of the fellows at the Faculty about you. I figured if you could get someone like me through my exams, you could tutor anybody. I know a few of them will be by to talk to you about it real soon.'

'That was very kind of you.' Harry blushed crimson as he stood in the doorway clutching his books and papers.

'Kind, hell,' he muttered. 'I wish I had a mind like yours. Just don't wanna see all that talent go to waste. Besides, I figured I owed you for all your help.' As he closed the door behind him, Gloria turned in time to see George emerging from their bedroom, a large handkerchief in his hand, his nose red and his voice husky.

'Can I come out now?'

'No one said you had to stay in the bedroom,' Gloria said, tidying the dining table.

'Didn't want to disturb your tutorial. Do you think he'll pass?'

'Probably.'

'So you'll have lots of new students, will you?'

'George, please.' Gloria stiffened.

'No, no – he's right. Why *should* all that talent go to

155

waste. Everybody', he observed after he had blown his nose vigorously, 'wants to help us out, don't they?'

Gloria put the back of her hand across his forehead. 'You still have a temperature, love. Why don't you go back to bed?' she asked, trying to lead him back towards the bedroom. He pulled away, heading for the door.

'I've felt worse. Where's my scarf?'

'Are you sure?' He opened the door and turned back to face her, the fever burning in two red spots in his cheeks.

'Exams start in two days, then it'll all be over, one way or the other.'

'Here,' Gloria said, grabbing her new pen out of its velvet case. 'Your pen keeps leaking all over your notes.' She offered it to him but he did not take it.

'You earned it. You keep it.'

'Why can't you just accept it?' Gloria cried. 'It might even bring you luck!' George turned away to head down the steps. 'Remember, Lionel is coming by for supper this evening,' she called after him. 'And before you ask me why he's coming, I don't know. He invited himself!' She heard the door to the street slam in the silence that followed her words.

'Why the suit?' Gloria asked Lionel as he sprawled across the couch in her living room. He was wearing a pin-striped three-piece despite the warmer weather and looked, as usual, elegant in it.

'Don't change the subject,' he chided. 'Have you shown these to George?' He grabbed a sheaf of letters from those Gloria kept in a file hidden in the bottom of a kitchen cupboard, and began to leaf through them.

'No,' she admitted, 'not yet. He hates the fact that I have to work to support us, so I thought I'd wait until he got his degree before telling him I was looking for a clerkship. It's pretty hopeless anyway,' she continued, reclaiming the letters from Lionel. 'I think I wrote to every law firm south of Newcastle.' She looked through the letters and chose some of them and put them aside.

'There's this one,' she said, beginning to read from it. ' *"We are a reputable firm and not in the habit of taking women into our employ "*. Or this one – I got several like this. *"Although we would not take you into chambers, we would consider you for a senior secretarial position should you have the requisite skills. "* Ah, now here,' she said, waving one of the letters at Lionel, 'is one that lifted my heart. They actually asked me to come and see them. They didn't mind that I was a colonial: they didn't mind that I was a woman – wonderful!' She smiled a small, bitter smile. 'They took one look at me, or rather, I took one look at their faces and I knew I had wasted the train-fare.' She shoved all the letters back into the folder and tied the cotton ribbon that bound it with short, jerky movements. 'Harry has sent some of his friends around to talk to me about tutoring them. Maybe that's what I should do.'

'You think you should give up the idea of practising law?' Lionel asked in a deceptively mild voice, examining his tie-pin closely.

'I prefer to call it compromise.'

'I never thought I'd see the pocket battleship becalmed,' he observed, stroking his tie into place. Just then, George's tread could be heard mounting the steps and Gloria rushed to stow her folder under the couch. She kicked the last corner of it out of sight just as the door opened to admit her husband.

'Sorry I'm late. I fell asleep in the stacks, I'm afraid. It's this stupid head cold.' He smiled ruefully at Lionel. 'I won't come too close in case it spreads to you.'

'Appreciate it.'

'Still feeling rotten?' Gloria asked, feeling his forehead.

'Like I've been run over by a Sherman tank,' George admitted.

'I'll put you to bed as soon as we've eaten,' Gloria decided.

'I have to go back to the library!' Lionel fell to studying his tie-pin again. The quivering silence held for a full minute.

'You won't be able to sit your stupid exams if you die of pneumonia,' Gloria said eventually. 'Lionel, please tell this man that discretion is the better part of valour!'

'I wouldn't argue with her, old man,' Lionel volunteered as he stood to face them both. 'Now be seated, both of you. Lionel has an important announcement to make. Hence the suit, you see, Gloria.'

'You finally met someone foolish enough to marry you?' George asked.

'Worse than that, I'm afraid. I'm sailing for home. Duty calls and all that,' he explained to a dismayed Gloria. 'I can't put it off any longer. The King of the Essequibo must return to his kingdom.'

'But what about your exams,' Gloria asked, trying hard to look composed.

'I'll leave as soon as they are over.'

'Is everything all right at home?' George enquired shrewdly. Lionel shrugged.

'The aged parent has fallen into decline, I'm afraid. The old lion's heart is failing. Time for me to take up those responsibilities I've spent the better part of my adult life avoiding.'

'It's going to be terribly quiet around here without you,' Gloria said, feeling silly at saying something so trite at such a time.

'Yes, it will,' George agreed.

'It's interesting,' Lionel mused, determined to break the silence that hung over them, 'how an announcement like this tends to create silences, isn't it? Did you ever think to see Gloria lost for words, George? Do you know, even *you* look subdued . . . though of course that could be the influenza!'

'Do you know exactly when you're leaving?' George asked, watching Gloria fight against the tears that had sprung to her eyes.

'Another fortnight or so,' Lionel said. 'The ticket should arrive any day now.'

'I find it extremely difficult to picture you anywhere else but striding along King's Parade,' Gloria said at last, managing a smile, although her voice trembled.

'What is it like, living in Guyana?' George asked as they sat down to dinner.

'I've known you for two years and this is the first time you've asked me that,' Lionel observed as he helped himself to neat portions of reconstituted mashed potatoes and beef shin stewed mercilessly until tender.

'Well, you just seem more at home in Cambridge than I do,' George confessed. 'It is a little surprising to think of you in a South American jungle somewhere.'

Lionel laughed. 'The only time I'll be in a jungle is when I go upcountry, hunting bird or agouti for sport. No, old bean, old sport, old son. I shall be confined to the substantial Georgetown offices of Ramkissoon & Son, pushing piles of paper across my desk and looking at the bottom line of long columns of profit and loss figures trying to see how best to make oodles of money with our gold, mahogany and sugar sales.'

'That,' said George, helping himself to more mash, 'seems entirely out of character for you.'

'If it was good enough for my father, it is good enough for me. Besides, it paid for me to be here all these years.'

They ate in silence, each occupied with their own thoughts, until Gloria looked across at Lionel and smiled ruefully.

'You'll be bored within two years,' she observed. 'You know you will.'

'Ah.' Lionel tidied his knife and fork and leaned back in his chair. 'I've thought about that. I've decided that after a suitable period of acclimatization, I shall get involved in politics.'

'Of course,' Gloria agreed, amused.

'Just like that?' George enquired.

'You have to understand that the West Indies is not like here. A man with a Cambridge degree cuts quite a figure there, and all sorts of doors are open to him. Besides, my dear George, tensions have been boiling beneath the surface for a long time in the Caribbean.' George looked to Gloria, who nodded. 'The colonial administrations are not popular and we are pretty sure we could do a better job of governing ourselves. A man like me could be very useful in that process.' Lionel rose from the table, taking their plates with him into the kitchen. 'After all, I have lived with the enemy. Who would know how to deal with the colonial administration better than a chap like me?'

'He'll probably end up in the Governor's mansion, George.'

'Why not?' Lionel said, returning to the table. 'I'm sure you could be just as useful in Jamaica, Gloria.' She shook her head warningly at Lionel – a movement George caught out of the corner of his eye.

'Don't be silly, Lionel!' Gloria scolded.

'Why is that silly?' George asked, looking from one to the other. 'I'm sure you could be very useful if we were living in the Caribbean.'

'Even if you don't like the idea of politics, there's talk of a new university, of legal reform, of drafting new constitutions even. Now that was a subject on which she would wax lyrical in her student days, George. She knows there's work for her to do in Jamaica.' Again George looked from one brown face to the other.

'Is that what she said to you?' George asked Lionel, who was studiously avoiding Gloria's glare.

'Lionel!' Gloria warned.

'Somebody has to talk plainly, my dear. It's what she has always wanted to be part of, George. Creating a new future.'

'Oh, for God's sake, be quiet, Lionel!' Gloria snapped.

'Instead,' George asked him, 'she is trapped here with me, tutoring overgrown Americans?'

'I am here because I want to be here, because this is where I belong!'

'And those are the horns of the dilemma on which she is impaled. The woman loves you, George. It's a hard fact, but you are just going to have to face it,' Lionel pontificated with gusto.

'I am warning you!' Gloria threatened, getting up from her seat, twisting her napkin into a short strap.

'See what I mean, old fellow,' Lionel demanded of George as he retreated to the end of the room. 'She fires a shot across my bow and I'm not even the enemy!'

'We used to talk about all the things you wanted to do back home in Jamaica when we first met,' George reminded his wife, standing strategically between her and Lionel and taking the napkin from her hands.

'That was then,' she replied. 'My life is with you now. May we please talk about something else?'

'I most certainly will,' Lionel agreed. He made his way back to the table and from a small satchel he had brought with him, he extracted a dusty bottle of white wine. He opened it and filled three mismatched glasses that George brought from the kitchen. 'I don't permit sentimental farewells, so let us just drink to friendship, the future and soon-to-be absent friends. Sorry, Gloria,' he continued after they had all drunk a toast, 'I had no right to stick my oar in, but I couldn't live with myself if I hadn't tried.'

CHAPTER FOURTEEN

Radnor   *12th June, 1947*
Half Way Tree Post Office
St Andrew

Dear Gloria,

You remember Mrs Milton? Both of her sons are at the LSE in London having worked downtown at the Colonial Office on King Street for a few years. Or was it with the Postmaster General? I can never remember. They have jobs waiting for them in the Civil Service here when they come home. I wondered if you had bumped into them?

Mrs Marley and I went to a political meeting the other evening. Very exciting, with the candidates for the election standing on the back of carts and flat-bed trucks, shouting above the singing of party songs. The one I liked best wore the nicest white suit and Panama hat and spoke about the need for better schools for poor children, and for stand-pipes to bring clean water. Very interesting, but we had to leave early because the crowd was getting very large and the police were beginning to look very impatient. Besides, it doesn't do to be seen at places like that too often. Not when your husband is on nodding terms with the Governor himself. I tell your father not to talk too loudly when he is telling people that he agrees with the politicians and what they are trying to do!

Do you realize it has been one whole year since you decided to throw your future away and get married? Six years since I laid eyes on my only child. I hope you are happy. At least one of us should be.

Mother

The clock on the mantelpiece ticked loudly in the dark room. Gloria, sitting on the couch and listening to the distant shouts of celebrating undergraduates along King's Parade, noticed how the sound kept eating into her thoughts, reminding her how close to midnight it was. She heard the door to the street go and opened the flat door just as George stumbled to the top of the steps. He blinked owlishly at her and steadied himself on the door jamb before entering the dark apartment.

'Where have you been?'

'Celebrating, my dear,' George answered. 'Celebrating. Going down in flames. Crashing and burning. That sort of thing.'

'Keep your voice down, George, please.'

'Why? Why should I?' His voice got louder and louder and he banged on the dining table at each word. 'You're not sleeping. I'm not sleeping. Why should I keep my bloody voice down?'

'Why don't we go to bed? We can talk in the morning,' Gloria suggested.

'Don't you want to know how my final exam went?' George demanded. 'And why the hell are you waiting here in the dark? Why the hell are we talking in the dark?' He threw the light switch and Gloria saw how flushed he was, how his face, slackened by beer, contorted in the overhead light. 'Don't you want to know how my final exam went? It was magnificent in its simplicity. There is a majesty to the blank page, a resonance to deep silence that is quite . . .' he paused, searching for the word '. . . indescribable.'

'How much have you had to drink, George?'

'After months of sitting around staring at books in cold libraries, I couldn't think of anything to write. Not one sentence, not one phrase, not even,' he told her, looking bewildered, 'one word. Nothing.'

The door to the bedroom opened and a plump figure swathed in a generous green chenille dressing gown entered the room. She pushed a handful of dyed red hair off a face that was beginning to show signs of wear and tear and shook her head.

'Look at you,' she said. 'Smelling like a brewery and swaying like a willow tree in a high wind. Is that any way to behave, George Compton?' She was amused to see her nephew's mouth fall open.

'Aunt Anne?' he squeaked. 'Gloria, this is my Aunt Anne.'

'I know, dear. We introduced ourselves when she arrived this afternoon.'

George felt an urgent need to sit down; he stumbled to the couch. 'What on earth is she doing here? She never comes to visit . . . you never come to visit, do you, Aunt Anne? What are you doing here?'

Aunt Anne searched around in the pocket of her dressing gown and fished out a pack of cigarettes.

'What do you *think* I'm doing here?' she asked, squinting at her nephew through the smoke exhaled from a hearty first draw. 'Welcoming my new niece into the family, that's what. And look what I come to find!'

'She arrived,' Gloria told George, 'this afternoon. I've invited her to stay.'

Aunt Anne's laugh rumbled up from her belly and carried everything before it. Gloria could not help joining in.

'You look a right fool, laddie, gawping at me with your mouth open like that,' Aunt Anne observed. 'What? Did you think everyone in your family was a sanctimonious old cow like your mam? Sitting around that house with her face all made up like she smelled something bad? Telling people she was too good to be associated with common folk – a barmaid like me? I got tired of asking Her Majesty when you were coming to visit and decided to come and visit you instead. I had to give that porter at your college what for to find out where you lived, but I was given this address and here I am. I've got two weeks' holiday,' she concluded, 'and as you didn't answer any of my letters, turning up out of the blue like this was the only way.'

'You never even opened them, did you, George?' Gloria reminded him. Her husband's mouth opened and shut several times before he could say anything intelligible.

'I'm utterly and completely flabbergasted,' he told them finally.

'And I'm deeply disappointed that you thought everyone in your family would hold the same foolish opinions as your mother. My brother must be spinning in his grave!'

'You heard about our disastrous visit then.'

'Heard, saw and had a few words with those who should have known better!' Aunt Anne declared.

'What on earth are *you* grinning at?' George demanded of Gloria.

'The expression on your face,' she explained gleefully.

'I've just failed one of my exams,' George declared with all the dignity he could muster, 'and come home to find my maiden aunt in residence. How should I look?'

'Maiden aunt?' Aunt Anne echoed, crowing with laughter. 'He means the black sheep of the family, Gloria – the black ewe! I guess that gives you and me something in common right there!'

'I don't think that is in the least amusing,' George declared as the two women fell about the flat.

'I think we've shocked the poor boy, love,' Aunt Anne chuckled, wiping the tears of laughter away with the sleeve of her dressing gown. 'That always was your problem, George, even as a little boy. Always wanting things to be just so. Always wanting things to be perfect. Saint George,' she teased him gently, 'charging at every dragon he sees.'

'How would you know? You never came to our house when I was a boy,' he retorted, looking exactly like a schoolboy.

'Your mother made sure of that! To this day, I'm convinced that she tricked my brother into marrying her. But I always knew what was going on in your life. I made sure his father told me whenever he sneaked into the pub where I worked for a pint before going home to Her Majesty, Gloria. That man loved you, George. Talked about you with such pride.'

'Well,' Gloria said, breaking the emotion-filled silence, 'as we are all awake and I think George is almost sober, shall I make us something hot to drink?'

'You just look in my small suitcase, love,' Aunt Anne ordered. 'You'll find a bottle of Mother's Ruin that will do me very nicely. I think,' she said, taking a bewildered George by the elbow and steering him to the couch, 'this young man and I have some talking to do!'

Gloria followed in Aunt Anne's wake as she sailed majestically through Cambridge market, her red hair standing out like a beacon among the stalls. Her cigarette hung either from her fingers or from the corner of her mouth as she examined each item she purchased with care before stowing it in her sturdy string bag.

'Just a few more spuds and I'll be finished here. Where do you usually buy them, Gloria?' she called over her shoulder.

'Down this way,' Gloria told her, guiding her down a narrow aisle between two rows of canvas tenting. 'Not the pleasantest man but he has the cheapest fruit and veg.'

'When did you last buy yourself a new frock?' Aunt Anne asked as they navigated around a pile of discarded cabbages.

'I don't worry about such things.'

'Not for a long time then,' Aunt Anne confirmed. 'I don't know how you and George manage in that draughty old place either.'

'Oh, it's not so bad,' Gloria said, pointing out a small stall to her companion. 'Especially now that the weather is warmer. The only thing I truly hate is having to stamp around before I open the cupboard so that the rats have time to clear out! Will two pounds of potatoes be enough?'

'George looks pale and you look thin,' the other woman observed. 'Two pounds of potatoes – and mind you don't give me anything but your best!' she warned the vendor, a thin man with equally thin hair which he scraped forward to hide a receding hairline. He sized up the two women with a cynical eye.

'Well, if it isn't my African Princess,' he said, as he weighed out the potatoes. Aunt Anne prised up the forefinger with which he seemed determined to weigh the scale down and he reluctantly added another tiny potato. 'Anything else for you, love?' he asked Gloria with a leer.

'I'll have some of those plums,' Aunt Anne said.

'What – no bananas?' the vendor sneered. 'Can't get no bananas, can we. You lot must have eaten them all, Princess. Bet it makes you lot hungry swinging around in them trees all day!' He handed Aunt Anne her purchases.

'What did you say?' Aunt Anne asked. She dropped her cigarette to the ground, crushing it under her heel before turning to face the vendor, arms crossed over her chest.

'It doesn't matter,' Gloria whispered, pulling her away.

'It bloody well matters to me,' Aunt Anne declared. 'Oy! You! I think you should apologize to this young woman!'

'D'you hear that, Pete?' the vendor shouted to the booth across the way. 'Some blousy old tart wants me to apologize! It was a joke, love. *A joke.* I always have a little joke with the African Princess when she comes for her produce, don't I, love? Just pay me what you owe and stop making a fool of yourself.'

'I'd rather eat sawdust than put money in your pocket!' Aunt Anne told him, tossing the potatoes and plums back at the vendor.

'Nobody sells them cheaper than me, love. The Princess knows that, don't you, love? She'll be back, won't you, Princess!' the vendor called after their retreating backs. His sallies were rewarded with some laughter from the other traders. Several of the shoppers stood and watched with open curiosity and some derision as the middle-aged spinster with the flaming red hair marched ahead of the small, dark woman out of the market.

'Do you have to put up with this all the time?' Aunt Anne demanded as soon as the market was out of sight.

'Most people aren't that bad,' Gloria assured her. 'It doesn't bother me.'

'Well, it makes me bloody angry,' Aunt Anne swore. 'Does George know about this?'

Gloria paused before she answered, not daring to look Aunt Anne in the eye. 'I look after the house,' she explained. 'That's the arrangement. He has been working so desperately hard this last year. It didn't seem right to tell him.'

Aunt Anne patted Gloria's cheek, her hands rough against her skin, then she lit another cigarette. 'You're willing to live through this for George?'

'He is losing far more than I am by marrying me, Aunt Anne. The truth is, whether or not I was married to George, as long as I live in England, these things will happen. It's not his fault.'

'Losing far more? Who told you that?'

Gloria glanced across at Aunt Anne as they turned into Botolph Lane. 'His tutor,' she admitted. 'In no uncertain terms. "George would have a solid future, maybe even a brilliant one"...' She imitated Dr Weekes's precise tones.

'Have you told George he said this to you?'

Again Gloria hesitated before answering. 'I didn't see the point,' she said eventually.

'It seems to me that you've both got yourselves into quite a little pickle,' Aunt Anne observed as they fetched up at the street door to the flat.

'My place is here with George.'

'Then why,' Aunt Anne quizzed her, 'are you so sad?'

Gloria opened the street door to find Lionel sitting, elbows on his knees, on the stairs to the flat.

'About time you got home, battleship,' he remonstrated, dusting off the seat of his trousers with a puce handkerchief as he stood up. 'The butcher let me in here, but I've been loitering with intent for a good fifteen minutes!' He took Aunt Anne's string bag and Gloria's few packages from them to carry them up the stairs.

'Lionel, this is George's aunt, Aunt Anne. Aunt Anne, this is a friend of ours, Lionel Ramkissoon. Shortly to return to the West Indies.'

'I set out tomorrow, I'm afraid. Just popped by to say farewell and such.'

'Just the man I want to speak to then,' Aunt Anne said, looking him over approvingly as they climbed the stairs. 'There's some things I want to know about the Comptons that only a good friend would know.'

'Sounds formidable,' Lionel remarked, making his way to the kitchen with their purchases.

'Aunt Anne *is* formidable,' Gloria told him. 'Aren't you, Aunt Anne?'

Easing herself onto the couch and shaking off her shoes, Aunt Anne wiggled her toes thoughtfully.

'A woman comes to a point in her life when she has no time to waste pretending she doesn't see what is going on under her nose. I like,' she concluded, 'to speak plainly.'

169

Lionel, grinning broadly, emerged from the kitchen. 'I think I'm in love,' he declared.

'And I think you are the most outrageous flirt – a man after my own heart. Come,' she said patting the cushion beside her, 'and let's have our little chat while I figure out how I am going to cook tea without any bleedin' potatoes!'

'Let me put this in context for you, Aunt Anne. There were nearly fifty of us doing our LLBs at the same time as Gloria. Two of that fifty got first-class honours. Our pocket battleship was one.'

'Yet she still can't find a job,' Aunt Anne mused.

'I tutored Harry,' Gloria insisted.

'Which is, Aunt Anne, like using an incendiary bomb to light a cigarette,' Lionel concluded.

'Right. So basically you two have been living off George's demob scholarship, his college prize – his Exhibition you call it? – and the money you make tutoring.'

'Enough, both of you!' Gloria said between annoyance and amusement. 'George and I will sort this out together. Thank you for your concern, but we are fine.'

'Hence the nickname, Aunt Anne,' Lionel confided.

Just then, they heard the sound of footsteps thundering up the stairs as George raced up them two at a time and burst breathlessly into the room.

'Well, which one do you want to hear first?' he demanded. 'The good news or the bad?'

'And what did the estimable Dr Weekes have to say?' Gloria asked.

'The same Dr Weekes you told me about?' Aunt Anne asked her, Gloria nodded.

'The bad news is that he says he doesn't see any way I can take my exams over, even if I stay up for the summer vac and prepare. I've had my chance,' George told them, looking curiously at his wife and his aunt.

'You knew he wanted you to give up trying to finish in one year, my love. He has always been furious about that. He won't do you any favours, even if he could.' Gloria's tone was bracing, but her eyes betrayed concern.

'And what was the good news?' Aunt Anne asked.

'Just look at that face!' Lionel chuckled. 'He's passed, ladies. You'll see – done better than pass!'

'Two one!' George announced, grinning broadly.

Gloria dived into his open arms. 'Oh, George, that's wonderful!'

'Not quite up to your standard, my dear, but it will do. It will definitely do!' said George.

Lionel came across and shook his hand energetically. Aunt Anne, smiling broadly, struggled up from her place on the couch and collected her string bag and her purse.

'I won't be a moment,' she said at the door.

'Where are you off to now?' George asked, surprised. 'I thought we were going to celebrate!'

'We are,' Aunt Anne assured him. 'I just need a few potatoes for the hot pot I am going to cook for us, and there's a man in the market. I want to give a piece of my mind to at the same time!' And she stumped firmly out of the door and down the steps.

George looked to Gloria, who shrugged, and Lionel, who grinned.

'Well, young people,' Lionel began, 'wonderful as Aunt Anne's hot pot sounds, it's time for me to shake your hands briskly and head out into the world.'

'Oh, Lionel.' Gloria's heart sank and she felt George's grip around her shoulders tighten bracingly.

'The stiff upper lip is not natural to my race,' Lionel continued, staring fixedly at a spot on the wall, 'so I am maintaining it with a good deal of effort. Goodbye, Comptons. You have provided a wastrel like me with a home away from home and a great friendship and I will be eternally grateful.'

'Don't talk rubbish. You know you were always welcome,' Gloria said, her voice husky.

Lionel managed a small smile as he extended a hand to George. 'I rehearsed that line all the way over here,' he said. 'And I was determined to say it. Look after one another,' he ordered, gripping George's hand tightly, 'and I shall expect you to come and visit me in Guyana some day.'

'Lionel, I wish you all the best,' George said, finding himself unwilling to let his hand go. 'May your boat sail on smooth seas . . .'

'I thank you.'

'. . . May your father be on the mend and happy to see you.'

'Again I thank you.'

'. . . And every now and then as you rake in your profits, may you spare a thought for those of us still here eking out our rationed existence.'

Lionel squared his shoulders, smiled as best he could and headed for the door. 'Absolutely. Of course. I shall now drag the remains of my dignity through the door and be off.'

George and Gloria stood together at the window and watched their friend tread firmly up the lane. He didn't look back, though they were sure he knew they were there. They had not expected him to look back.

'I shall miss him terribly,' Gloria whispered.

'We both shall,' George agreed. 'We both shall.'

'Not just his great friendship, George – not just that. You see, he was West Indian, like I am. I guess it was like having a kind of mirror. You know you exist because you can see something of yourself in it.'

'Is that how you really feel?'

'Part of me,' Gloria said, turning to face him. 'But only part of me.' She stroked his cheek then moved away from the window and began arranging the cushions on the couch. 'So, you got an upper second without even writing all the exams, did you?' she asked. 'Show-off!'

'Oh well,' George replied, 'anybody can get a first if they have the time!' He ducked as a well-aimed cushion sailed towards him.

'Have I told you lately that I think you are absolutely brilliant?' Gloria asked.

'What was that?' George said, advancing on her. 'I seem to be having some trouble picking that up.'

'Absolutely,' Gloria said, crawling across the couch towards him, 'BRILLIANT.'

'You're going to have to come closer, I'm afraid,' George sighed, settling himself on the middle of the couch. 'I just can't seem to make out what you are saying.'

'Is this close enough?'

'I don't know,' George said, pulling her down to lie beside him. 'Say it again and let's see.'

'Absolutely,' Gloria whispered, 'brill . . .'

'Yes,' George replied a few minutes later as their first kiss ended and they were fumbling at buttons and laces, 'I think I heard it that time.'

Aunt Anne closed her knife and fork, lit a cigarette, then tapped on her glass with her dessert spoon. The summer-evening light still lingered in the sky outside and made the flat look a welcoming place, full of soft shadows. Gloria, George and Aunt Annie sat at the dining table in a pool of light from a fat tallow candle.

'Right, you two, I have an announcement to make,' she declared. 'First of all, congratulations to my nephew George for not only being the first Compton to go to university, but for doing it in such style. Cambridge, no less, and an upper second to boot.'

'I thank you,' George said, raising a glass of Pimms Punch, their celebratory extravagance, to his aunt.

'More importantly, I wanted to congratulate him on his choice of wife.'

'Hear, hear,' Gloria chimed in.

'I have a small confession to make to you, Gloria. I came down here to look you over. Having said that, it took me about five minutes to decide that you were just the ticket.'

'Hear, hear!' George roared.

'Be quiet, you!' Aunt Anne ordered. 'Now, here comes the important bit.'

'You've decided to move down to Cambridge and feed us up on your hot pot?'

'No, I've made a decision. When your dad died, George, he left something to me after he made sure your mother would be well looked after. He was a good man, that way.'

'Rest in peace, Father.' George raised a glass again.

'Amen. I've decided that I want to give that money to you both.'

In the pin-drop silence that followed, George and Gloria exchanged glances.

'Absolutely not,' George finally responded. 'We would never dream of accepting it.'

'It was a lovely thought but we really don't need—' Gloria began, but Aunt Anne cut her short.

'Don't need it? I knew you were going to say that. His father was like that too, Gloria. Never once admitted anything was wrong. Kept it all inside. Died too young because of it.'

'If Dad left that money for you . . .' George pointed out in his most reasonable tone.

'George, I am a working woman. I have a room at the pub that costs me nothing. I have neither chick nor child to spend it on. That money would just carry on sitting in the bank, making nobody any the happier. Besides, I am giving you the money on one condition.'

'Now I know you are my father's sister,' George chuckled.

'It is time you went and visited your in-laws in Jamaica.'

Gloria felt her heart begin to race, her throat begin to tighten. Her eyes flew to her husband's face.

'Do you know how much that would cost, Aunt Anne?' he demanded. 'No, I can't possibly allow you to—'

'Allow? You're saying that I have to get your permission to give you a gift?'

'No,' George admitted, caught on the back foot. Aunt Anne got up from the table and fetched Gloria's folder from the kitchen cupboard. She set it down on the table in front of her nephew and opened it.

'Has Gloria showed you these?'

George looked at his wife, who sat stock-still staring at the letters Aunt Anne was shoving under his nose.

'Look – read! She's been trying to find someone who will take her into chambers, George. Lionel explained it all to me. I went to the market with her today. Someone thought it was a joke to say that people like her spend their time swinging through the trees. Have you any idea what her life is like from day to day?'

Gloria felt a wave of panic overwhelming her, dragging her into a powerful sea she had until this moment spent much of her time and energy avoiding.

'Aunt Anne, please . . .' she whispered.

'Gloria?' George asked, sounding puzzled. 'Is this true?'

'That's their ignorance,' she said, knowing that she sounded like a schoolchild reciting by rote what it is taught to say. 'It doesn't bother me.'

'You had your head buried so deep in those books of yours, you didn't see what was right in front of your nose. Do you know what she worries about, George?' Gloria felt a physical pain at the bewildered look on his face. 'That being married to her will hold you back. That one day you won't want to have her around!'

The tears crashed over the seawall against Gloria's will.

'Aunt Anne, don't,' she heard herself pleading in a voice that sounded distant and strange even to her own ears.

'I'm a barmaid, remember. There isn't too much in the way of human misery that I haven't heard or seen!'

'I have to find a job, find us somewhere to live,' George started to say, but his eyes were riveted to his wife's face. It is as if a mask has been cruelly ripped away, he thought to himself, and I am made suddenly aware how little I actually saw of what was really there.

'For heaven's sake,' Aunt Anne snapped, pulling a handkerchief out of her capacious bosom and handing it to Gloria, 'will you just listen to yourself? *You* have to, *you* must . . . *No*, George! *You* don't have to do anything but go to Jamaica. Take the gift and go!'

'I have to think about it,' George said, treading water.

'No, you don't. I've found out how much the tickets are, and when the ship sails. What you need to do is ask your wife what she wants to do!'

'Gloria?'

'Tell him how you really feel, my darling. He's a grown man.'

For a heartbeat, Gloria remembered the moment when at fourteen years old she had arrived at Mary Datchelor, stood at the school gates and heard her mother tell her to stand up straight and look the world in the eye. She drew a deep, steadying breath and took George's hand.

'I would love to go home, just for a while. It's been six years since I saw my family and friends. Yes, I would love to go home.'

'I . . .' George began.

'There you go with that "I" again!' his aunt snapped.

'I . . . would like to say thank you very much, Aunt Anne.' George was surprised to see his aunt completely overwhelmed. She put her head in her hands and sat very still for a moment. When she looked up again, her eyes glittered with unshed tears and her face was wreathed in the broadest smile George had ever seen. Gloria got up from her seat and planted a kiss on Aunt Anne's beaming face.

'About time!' the older woman said, groping fruitlessly in her bosom for her handkerchief. 'Good Lord, I envy you. Sunshine and sea-bathing . . .'

'No rationing!' Gloria sang out.

'You sail from Southampton in a week's time, so you'd better start packing,' Aunt Anne told them. 'Surprised you, haven't I, nephew?'

'Completely!' George agreed.

'I wish your mother could be here to see all this!' Aunt Anne crowed, stubbing out her cigarette. 'She'd probably organize to have me burnt at the stake! Right, anyone for seconds?' she asked, opening the lid of the still warm hot pot and letting the fragrance of it escape into the room.

&PILOGUE

GEORGE DODGED THROUGH the traffic to cross the Half
Way Tree road and slipped into the cool shadows of the
Chinese shop on the other side of the road. Chang's Emporium smelled of saltfish and a barrel of it stood in the corner
nearest the counter. It's top was scarred by the vigorous blows
of the cleaver wielded by Mr Chang or his wife as they divided
off just as much of the fish as their customers needed to buy.
That was, George thought to himself, the beauty of this shop.
You could buy a penny's worth of salty butter and carry it
home sweating gently in its brown paper wrapping. Or half a
dozen paradise plum sweets to go with that pint of lamp oil or
kerosene you'd really come into the shop to get. Sacks of red
peas, rice, cornmeal and flour lined the walls like lazy soldiers
while, from the shelves above, carbolic soap and macassar oil
added to the rich tapestry of smells. The valuable items
including the bottles of red and white rum that lined the walls
behind the sturdy wooden counter. Trays of coconut sweets
and bullah cakes smiled at customers from within glass
topped boxes.

'Mornin'.' Mr Chang stood arms folded behind the
counter.

'Cigarettes, please. Six,' George explained.

Mr Chang set about taking the cigarettes out of the pack
and rolling them expertly in a twist of brown paper without
making eye contact.

'How Missa Carter?'

Mr Chang, like all the other many residents and business
people around Half Way Tree knew Will Carter, knew and

178

respected him. He owned several houses and blocks of flats in the area and was proprieter of the gas station right across the road from the Emporium where George was currently employed.

'Doing well.' George responded, searching in his trouser pockets for the money to pay for his cigarettes.

'Put them on tick?' Mr Chang asked, the edges of his mouth turned down with disapproval.

'No. No, I have . . .' George searched the pockets of his shirt. The sweat that frequently drenched him since coming to live in Jamaica, started to drip from his forehead again. As he took out his handkerchief to mop it up, several coins fell to the ground. He dived for them, retrieving them with relief then handed them to a still unsmiling Mr Chang.

It had not been a good day. The petrol delivery had been late and irate drivers had crowded the forecourt for a good couple of hours that morning. It had not helped that his father-in-law had sorted the situation in fifteen minutes with one phone call and an invitation to key customers to join him in the office. Grateful as he was for any job, George often felt something tighten in his chest when he contemplated his life.

After a year and more, he and Gloria were still living with his in laws. Much as he liked the house with the polished wooden floors and continual quiet bustle of household activity, so different from the cramped two up two down he grew up in, he had also come to feel confined by it. Gloria had got herself a job working with the Extra Mural department of the newly established University College of the West Indies and she loved her job. The brightest and best from all over the Caribbean had gathered on the newly built campus and she came home every day with tales of some idea, some issue, some poem or essay that she had been discussing with her students. He did his best to sound interested, to be happy for her, but he knew that she saw it when he could not school his face into the right expression, or heard when some sliver of bitterness threaded its way through his response.

Unable to face the gas station quite yet, he lit a cigarette and lingered by the doors of the shop for the first few calming draws.

'Dat white boy marry Missa Carpenter daughter sake of him money,' he heard Mr Chang say. His wife's response was too muffled for George to hear. 'Yes, but she could do better than him,' Mr Chang said.

With a good solid case of the blue devils to contend with, George turned away from the station and walked towards home. As he turned in the gate, he saw Mother sitting on the verandah, sewing basket in her lap, snipping off a length of embroidery thread from a skein. Gloria came out to join her, kicking off her shoes and sitting cross-legged. She was talking animatedly, the two women enjoying each other's company. George slipped across the lawn towards the large mango tree at the side of the house. Leaning against the trunk, cigarette in hand, George thought about England. He had been doing it more and more recently. Yes, there was rationing and life would never be so plump as it was here in Jamaica. But how can I appreciate such constant greenery when there is no winter with which to contrast it? How can I make my way in the world when I can't seem to find a direction to go in?

Distracted by such thoughts, he did not hear Gloria's approach.

'That cigarette is going to give your finger a nasty burn,' she observed. George put it out. 'I don't think Mother saw you sneak around here so you're safe for a while,' she added.

George could not think of what to say so he said nothing.

'Father called. Asking where you were. I said you were not feeling well.'

George still did not know what to say.

'Is it so dreadful?' Gloria asked.

'Not dreadful at all. That's the trouble. If I were a different man, I would be crowing how clever I was to fall on my feet like this.'

'Come.' Gloria held out her hand to George. 'Come. I have something to show you.'

As soon as Gloria put the nose of the Austin up the hill, it began to hesitate. The gears clashed loudly as she put it into second. After a moment or two, it began to haul itself up the road.

'Long Lane. Steeper than it looks,' Gloria told George. 'Don't look so worried. We'll soon be there.'

They drove in silence, Gloria concentrating hard on her driving. The road wound up into the hills to the north of Kingston. Outcrops of pink limestone and sudden deep valleys filled with cedar and flame of the forest trees came and went. The air grew cooler and George, almost against his will, felt the tensions of the day drain away.

Gloria drew the car to the halt at the side of the road.

'Up there,' she said. All George could see was a narrow, stony path leading up the side of a hill, the vegetation growing so close that he could not see where it led. 'Come on.'

'What do you think?' Gloria puffed a few minutes later.

The river plain on which Kingston sprawled lay before him. Deep valleys thick with vegetation sloped down from where he stood. Beyond the plains, the harbour glittered in the late evening sun. A cicada began its contagious song and soon George's head was ringing with the insect's sound. Ground doves disturbed by their approach, settled into the cedar trees behind them, cooing and flapping.

'I found it when I was helping father with his papers. He

didn't even remember he had bought it. It's ours. Or it will be. I'm buying it from him.'

'Because?' George enquired, trying hard not to show how stung he was that she had neither asked his advice or needed his help.

'We need our own home. Just you and I.'

Again George could not find the words.

'And there is something else,' she said. I wanted to give you this here, away from everybody else.'

Gloria took a brown envelope from the pocket of her dress and gave it to him.

'I snuck over to the registry and persuaded them to let me have it. I know I should have let them post it but I couldn't bear to wait.' She handed him the letter.

He handed it back to her. 'You read it for me,' he said.

'It's my turn to be brave, is it?' she teased. Gloria tore open the envelope and read the letter then kissed George gently on the cheek.

'Was that congratulations or commiseration?' he finally asked. She handed him the letter.

'Lecturer,' she said. 'Department of Economics, University College of the West Indies. You start next term.'

Their celebrations re-launched the ground doves and silenced the cicadas. Suddenly the full beauty of the view they had before them hit George. As it grew darker, street lights snaked across the plain. The shadows of the valleys grew velvet deep. For the first time since he had come to live in Jamaica, on this hillside, the promise of a real future in his hand, George felt at home. He reached for Gloria and pulled her close.

'You're shaking,'

'A little,' George admitted.

'Why?' Gloria scanned his face in the shadows. He thought

he had hidden it all so well, and who was she to take that away from him?

'It doesn't matter now. Our life has started, really started, and that's all that counts.'

THE END

Joan Blaney & Richard Scase

From Kitchen Sink to Boardroom Table

'A remarkable book' – Baroness Betty Boothroyd, *House of Lords*

'The sheer determination of these normal women to turn a raw deal into a good one leaves one humbled and inspired. They remind us all that lateral thinking and courageous endeavour can turn a potential victim into a confident and optimistic survivor. This book delighted me' – *Joanna Lumley*

'A moving and empowering collection of true stories which will inspire women of all ages and backgrounds' – *Juliette Foster, Sky News*

This will empower women to release their potential for corporate success and allow them to build on the skills they have developed managing the home and the family. An inspirational book, it demonstrates how women have the power and courage to deal with situations in the face of adversity.

Through real-life accounts that capture the essence of women's flexibility and foresight, *From Kitchen Sink to Boardrooom Table* features women from varied walks of life and shows how their personal and domestic skills can and have been harnessed into profitable and valued leading roles in modern day business. The key skills of financial and time management, team building and negotiation and the innate strength and courage of women from different backgrounds are revealed through inspirational stories. These two distinguished authors triumphantly show us that learning can be drawn from the most unexpected places and circumstances.

Paul Dash

Foreday Morning

'Dash uses delicate but vivid brushstrokes as he evokes his life in Barbados and Britain' – *Birmingham Evening Mail*

More than just an autobiography, it is a multi-faceted story that examines the tensions of race and colour in the colonial Caribbean and modern Britain

Paul Dash is one of Britain's leading academics and also a renowned painter. Born in Barbados, he came to Britain with his family at the age of eleven in the 1950s. *Foreday Morning* is the autobiography of a remarkable man who grew up with the influence of these two cultures.

Turning his artist's palette to his text, Dash reconstructs the cultural spaces in which black people lived in a colonial environment and which denigrated African heritages and venerated Western values. He then poignantly depicts the effect of seeing whites as the working class, sometimes living in poverty and ignorance, when he migrated to Britain. He examines the psychological repositioning required and his subsequent years of adjustment.

Dash explores his experiences as artist and educator and examines the lack of representation of Caribbean peoples in the British educational system.

Paul Crooks

Ancestors

'A moving account of a black British family that travels through the ages from slavery and beyond.' – *The Guardian*

'Groundbreaking. A riveting read.' – *Pride*

'An inspiring piece of literature.' – *The Voice*

Exceptional début novel. Highly recommended for the whole family.' – *Woman 2 Woman*

A gripping story of the author's own search for his family tree, which had been cruelly uprooted 300 years ago by the inhumanity of slavery. In the early 1990s Paul Crooks undertook an amazing journey from suburban North London to the Caribbean and from there to the Gold Coast of Africa where his story originally began. His journey to trace his lost ancestors is the gripping theme of this novel – fiction based on terrible fact . . .

In the late eighteenth century, August a boy of ten, meets Ami on the nightmare journey on board a slave ship from West Africa bound for Jamaica and she soon becomes his surrogate mother. Ami cares for August during the voyage and the novel tells the story of Ami and August's part in the struggle for emancipation and how he later becomes her son-in-law.

Po Wah Lam

The Locust Hunter

'A sprightly tale that captures the magical quality of Michael Ende's *The Neverending Story*. Recommended.' – *Time Out*

'Deceptively simple. A finely-wrought sculpture of a story that opens in the hand like a flower.' – *Publishing News*

Western ideals of rationality are pitted against the magic realism of Chinese folklore

The Locust Hunter, set in the humid and turbulent landscape of 1970s Hong Kong, is a coming of age tale that follows the journey of Sundance and his five friends, as they try to avenge the killing of the local 200-year-old pet tortoise, Lord Baltimore. Their village, encamped between the Big Amber (China) and the looming presence of the British Army, teeters precariously between colonial ideals and the teachings of Tao and Chinese customs. At the heart of the story is the contest held every 30 years to find the most proficient locust hunter in Hong Kong. Since time immemorial, the prize has been won by a member of the leading Triad family . . . who use every dirty trick in the book. Summoning all his young courage and his belief in life, 9-year-old Sundance takes them on – and wins.

Lakshmi Persaud

Raise the Lanterns High

A dramatic page turner, and a rich visual treat full of powerful ideas expressed in equally powerful language, with universal appeal. And at its heart is the image of burning, which ensures that the intellectual and emotional temperature never drops. It is a battle between the sexes, the conflict between modernity and long-honoured traditions, beautifully written with a pithy, punchy style.

On the eve of her wedding, Vasti finds her arranged marriage is to the rapist she saw in a sugarcane field years earlier. She can either speak out, defy convention and publicly disgrace her family or succumb to tradition and submit to her fate silently. The conflict rages within her and makes her ill, she collapses unconscious and is transported to the kingdom of Jyotika, two hundred years before where the three widowed queens of King Paresh are expected to climb onto a burning pyre to die with their dead husband, to perform the *sati* or widow burning. *Raise the Lanterns High* explores such cultural violations with compassion and drama, from the perspective of the women asked to make these impossible sacrifices, and shows the bravery required to accept as well as to reject these traditions. This is the story of female emancipation as harrowing as it is beautiful.

Mounsi
(Translated from the French by Lulu Norman)

The Demented Dance

'An excellent translation from the French' – *Banipal*

'A gripping tale of brutalised youth infused with a dark poetry' – *The Bookseller*

'Check out Mounsi's writing for yourself; it's a true lesson in walking in another's shoes' – *Time Out* book of the week

'A powerfully written novel about outcast adolescents' – *Publishing News*

'The novel speaks for all the uprooted people of France's inner cities' – *Le Monde*

Set in modern day France. This is the story of the marginal, desolate life of a young boy, Tarik, who exists on the edge of society. His life is so bleak that he is not even sure if he is really alive. His father, an Algerian factory worker and an alcoholic, loses his job, then gradually becomes mentally unbalanced, to the point where Tarik is taken into care. Shortly after this, Tarik starts to steal, take cars for joyrides and associate with other cast-off children. He and his friend Bako end up in borstal after a raid which culminates in murder. When Tarik is released he tries to go straight, falls in with various hustlers operating in Parisian society, becomes an escort and falls in love with Lise – who is very different to the other women he meets. Their relationship ends and Tarik moves in with Bako and Fania, who is on the game. When Fania dies of a smack overdose, Tarik and Bako, accompanied by Fania's cat, drive to the sea to scatter her ashes, with fatal consequences.

All BlackAmber Books are available from your local bookshop.

From a regular update on BlackAmber's lates release, with extracts, reviews and events, visit:

www.blackamber.com